RAND MCNALLY

kids' road atlas

BACKSEAT BOOKS®

UTAH

Bountiful
Salt Lake City
32
Kamas
Murray
Heber City
LAGOON AMUS. PARK
Salt Lake
189
OGOS ON.
velt

Table of Contents

Using an Atlas 4

United States 6

Washington, D.C. 7

Alabama 8

Alaska 9

Arizona 10

Arkansas 11

California.........................12

Colorado 14

Connecticut.....................15

Delaware..........................16

Florida 17

Georgia 18

Hawaii 19

Idaho 20

Illinois.........................21

Indiana 22

Iowa 24

Kansas 25

Kentucky 26

Louisiana 27

Maine 28

Maryland......................29

Massachusetts...............30

Michigan 32

Minnesota....................33

Mississippi 34

Missouri.......................35

Montana 36

Nebraska......................37

Nevada 38

New Hampshire 39

New Jersey 40

New Mexico 41

New York 42

North Carolina 44

North Dakota 45

Ohio............................46

Oklahoma 48

Oregon 49

Pennsylvania...................50

Rhode Island....................51

South Carolina 52

South Dakota 53

Tennessee 54

Texas 56

Utah.............................58

Vermont 59

Virginia 60

Washington 62

West Virginia 63

Wisconsin 64

Wyoming 65

Canada 66

Mexico..........................68

License Plate Game 70

Answers.........................71

Index 75

Using an Atlas...

Adventure or Mystery?

Is map reading an adventure or a mystery? It's only a mystery if you haven't uncovered the clues and codes. The information below will help you unlock the mystery and get started on the adventure. Solve the clues and use the numbered letters to fill in the secret message. For some of the clues you'll need to use the legend, scale, and coordinates, but for others you'll have to do a bit more detective work. Take a closer look at the maps for familiar cities, bordering states, and other details to help you find the answers. Good luck!

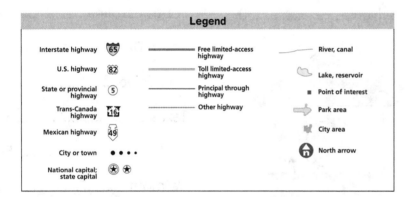

Legend

The legend, or map key, is a description of the symbols and lines on the map. Use the legend at the left for all of the maps in *Kids' Road Atlas*.

Clue #1: What National Park is at the southernmost section of the map at the right?

___ ___ ___ ___ ___ ___ ___ ___ ___ ___ National Park
             1   2

Clue #2: In what state will you find this park?

___ ___ ___ ___ ' ___ ___ ___
        3 4

Scale

Maps come in all sizes; some show the whole world and others show only a small neighborhood. The map scale tells you how space on a map equals distance on the earth. Scale is used to measure distances between places on a map. Measure the length of the distance from place to place on the map and then use the scale to find out how many miles or kilometers that is. The maps in *Kids' Road Atlas* are not all at the same scale, so be sure to look at the scale on each map to measure distance correctly.

Clue #3: On the map at the right, what "mile-high" city is approximately 30 miles southeast of Boulder on Interstate 70?

___ ___ ___ ___ ___ ___
   5   6

Clue #4: In what state will you find these two cities?

___ ___ ___ ___ ___ ___ ___ ___
   7   8

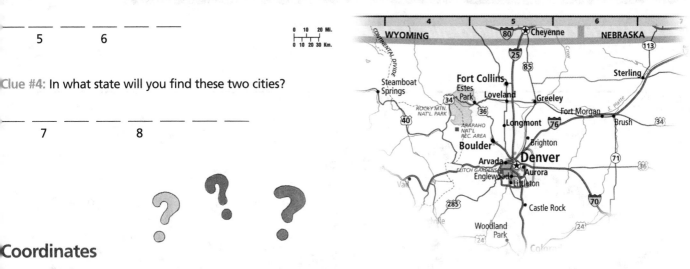

Coordinates

A coordinate is a letter–number combination that helps you find places on a map. To locate a city, look in the index to find the coordinate for that city. If, for example, the coordinate for the city is B–5, look down the right or left edge of the map for the letter B and draw an imaginary line across the map. Then, look across the top or bottom of the map for the number 5 and draw an imaginary line down or up until it crosses the imaginary line drawn from the letter B. The city will be inside the area around this point. For each map in the *Kids' Road Atlas* there is a yellow coordinate border with letters and numbers.

Clue #5: What coastal city on the map below is at coordinate I–6? Hint: There are several, so make sure you pick the one that fits in the blanks.

___ ___ ___ ___ ___ ___ ___ ___ ___ ___ ___
   9   10   11   12

Clue #6: In what state is this city?

___ ___ ___ ___ ___ ___ ___ ___ ___ ___
                13   14

Clue #7: You'll find this Mexican city at coordinate J–6.

___ ___ ___ ___ ___ ___ ___
15   16   17

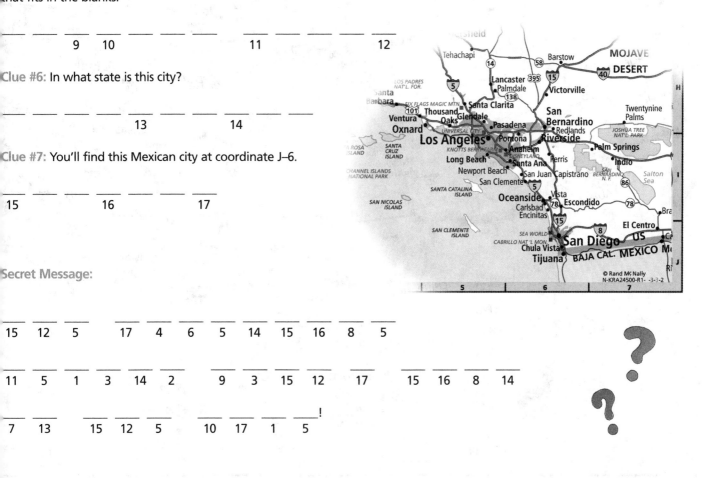

Secret Message:

___ ___ ___   ___ ___ ___ ___ ___ ___ ___ ___ ___
15 12   5   17   4   6   5 14 15 16   8   5

___ ___ ___ ___ ___ ___   ___ ___ ___ ___ ___   ___ ___ ___ ___
11   5   1   3 14   2   9   3 15 12 17   15 16   8 14

___ ___   ___ ___ ___   ___ ___ ___ ___ ___!
 7 13   15 12   5   10 17   1   5

United States

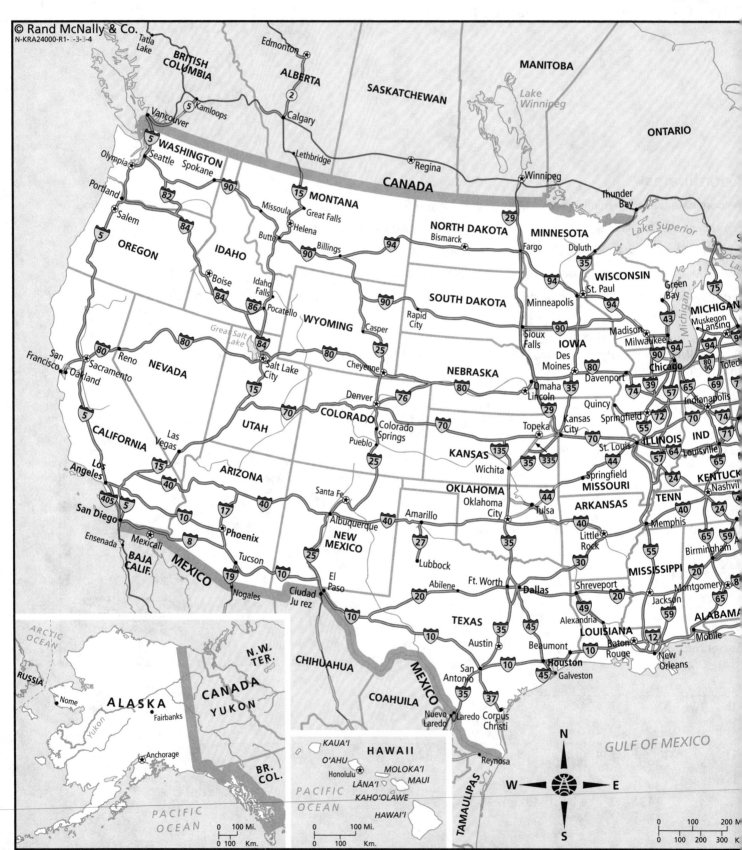

Tatla Lake
Edmonton
BRITISH COLUMBIA
ALBERTA
SASKATCHEWAN
MANITOBA
ONTARIO
Lake Winnipeg
Kamloops
Vancouver
Calgary
2
Lethbridge
Regina
Winnipeg
Thunder Bay
Lake Superior
Olympia
WASHINGTON
Seattle Spokane
Portland
82
90
15 MONTANA
Great Falls
NORTH DAKOTA
Bismarck
29
MINNESOTA
Fargo
Duluth
Salem
84
Missoula
Helena
Butte
90
Billings
35
WISCONSIN
Green Bay
75
MICHIGAN
Muskegon
Lansing
OREGON
5
IDAHO
Boise
Idaho Falls
86
Pocatello
WYOMING
90
SOUTH DAKOTA
Rapid City
94
SOUTH DAKOTA
94
St. Paul
Minneapolis
Madison
Milwaukee
43
94
94
84
Great Salt Lake
Casper
25
Cheyenne
NEBRASKA
Sioux Falls
IOWA
Des Moines
80
Chicago
80 90
Toledo
San Francisco
80
Reno
Sacramento
Oakland
NEVADA
Salt Lake City
15
80
Denver
76
80
Omaha
Lincoln
35
Davenport
74 39
57 65
69
70
74
Quincy
Springfield
55
INDIANA
Indianapolis
CALIFORNIA
Las Vegas
UTAH
70
COLORADO
Colorado Springs
Pueblo
KANSAS
Topeka
Kansas City
72
70
71
St. Louis
ILLINOIS
64
Louisville
5
Los Angeles
15
ARIZONA
40
25
135
Wichita
335
35
44
57
65
KENTUCKY
Nashville
24
405 5
San Diego
17
40
Santa Fe
Albuquerque
40
OKLAHOMA
Oklahoma City
Tulsa
44
MISSOURI
Springfield
ARKANSAS
TENN
Memphis
40
24
Ensenada
Mexicali
10
Phoenix
BAJA CALIF.
MEXICO
8
Tucson
NEW MEXICO
25
Amarillo
27
Lubbock
35
Little Rock
30
65 59
Birmingham
55
MISSISSIPPI
20
Montgomery
Jackson
65
ALABAMA
19
Nogales
10
Ciudad Juárez
El Paso
20
Abilene
Ft. Worth
Dallas
Shreveport
49
59
20
CHIHUAHUA
TEXAS
10
35
Austin
45
Beaumont
Houston
10
LOUISIANA
Baton Rouge
12
Mobile
New Orleans
COAHUILA
MEXICO
San Antonio
35
45
Galveston
37
Nuevo Laredo
Laredo Corpus Christi
Reynosa
TAMAULIPAS
GULF OF MEXICO

ARCTIC OCEAN
RUSSIA
N.W. TER.
CANADA YUKON
Nome
ALASKA
Fairbanks
Anchorage
BR. COL.
Yukon
PACIFIC OCEAN
0 100 Mi.
0 100 Km.

KAUA'I
O'AHU
Honolulu
HAWAII
MOLOKA'I
LĀNA'I MAUI
KAHO'OLAWE
PACIFIC OCEAN
HAWAI'I
0 100 Mi.
0 100 Km.

N
W E
S
0 100 200 Mi.
0 100 200 300 Km.

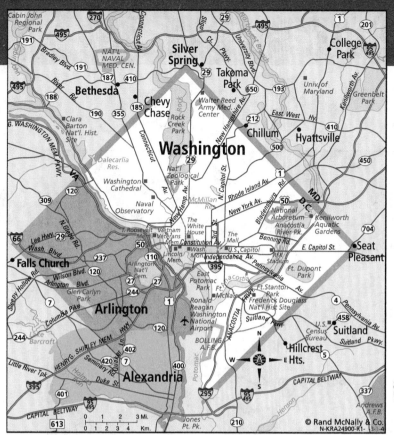

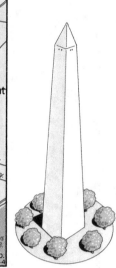

KEEP IT BRIEF

Each state has a two-letter abbreviation. Write the abbreviation for each state name in the blanks below. Remember that the two-letter abbreviation should be written in capital letters. Hint: Check out the state names in the red bar at the top of the pages in the book. The two letters of the abbreviation are the two capital letters in the name.

1. Alabama _____	18. Louisiana _____	35. Ohio _____
2. Alaska _____	19. Maine _____	36. Oklahoma _____
3. Arizona _____	20. Maryland _____	37. Oregon _____
4. Arkansas _____	21. Massachusetts _____	38. Pennsylvania _____
5. California _____	22. Michigan _____	39. Rhode Island _____
6. Colorado _____	23. Minnesota _____	40. South Carolina _____
7. Connecticut _____	24. Mississippi _____	41. South Dakota _____
8. Delaware _____	25. Missouri _____	42. Tennessee _____
9. Florida _____	26. Montana _____	43. Texas _____
10. Georgia _____	27. Nebraska _____	44. Utah _____
11. Hawaii _____	28. Nevada _____	45. Vermont _____
12. Idaho _____	29. New Hampshire _____	46. Virginia _____
13. Illinois _____	30. New Jersey _____	47. Washington _____
14. Indiana _____	31. New Mexico _____	48. West Virginia _____
15. Iowa _____	32. New York _____	49. Wisconsin _____
16. Kansas _____	33. North Carolina _____	50. Wyoming _____
17. Kentucky	34. North Dakota _____	

ALabama

Southern Pine

Camellia

Yellowhammer

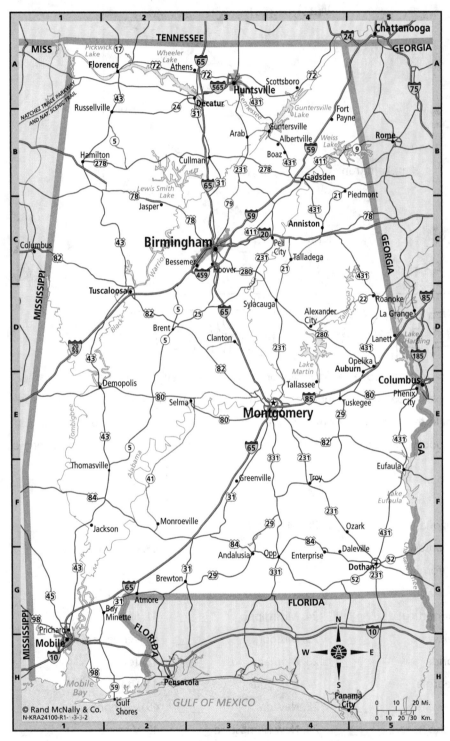

BLAST OFF!

Use the code to discover where the Space and Rocket Center is located. Write the letters in the blanks below.

A   B   E   H   I   L

M   N   S   T   U   V

8

AlasKa

Nickname: **The Last Frontier**

Capital: **Juneau**

Sitka Spruce | Forget-me-not | Willow Ptarmigan

DISCOVERING ALASKA

Circle the Alaska words in the grid below.

ANCHORAGE	IGLOO	SALMON
BALD EAGLE	JUNEAU	SNOW
DOG SLED RACE	KAYAK	TREE
ESKIMO	MOOSE	TUNDRA
GLACIER	MOUNTAIN	WATERFALL
GOLD	OTTER	WHALE
GRIZZLY BEAR	REINDEER	

```
K L L A F R E T A W M O
B A L D E A G L E S O A
S U Y L T R E E N L O N
R A E A T D L O G O S C
E E L S K N W I L M E H
E N G M O U N T A I N O
D U O T O T O A C K L R
N J A S K N T A I S S A
I O O W H A L E E E N G
E D O G S L E D R A C E
R A E B Y L Z Z I R G X
```

9

ARiZona

Palo Verde	Saguaro Cactus Blossom	Cactus Wren

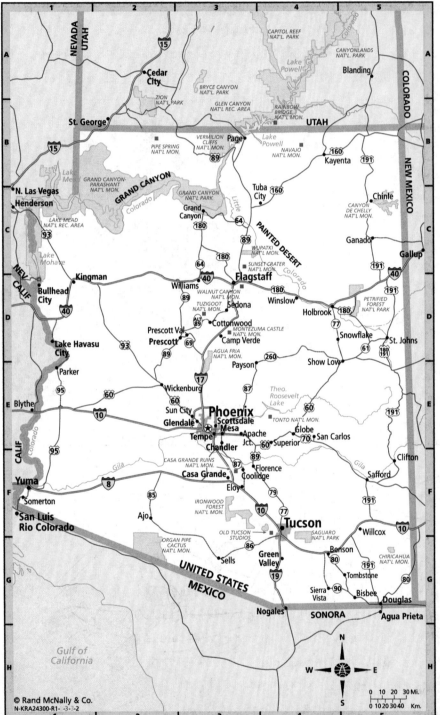

© Rand McNally & Co.
N-KRA24300-R1- -3-3-2

MIGHTY GRAND

The Grand Canyon (C–2) is one of the seven natural wonders of the world and its size is incredible. Solve the problems to find out just how big it is.

How Deep?

The Grand Canyon could fit <u>this many</u> Empire State Buildings inside its walls, stacked on top of one another!

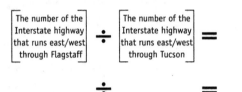

The number of the Interstate highway that runs east/west through Flagstaff	÷	The number of the Interstate highway that runs east/west through Tucson	=

$$\underline{\hspace{2cm}} \div \underline{\hspace{2cm}} = \underline{\hspace{2cm}}$$

How Long?

The Grand Canyon is <u>this many</u> miles long, almost the same as the width of the state of Illinois!

The number of the U.S. highway that runs down Arizona's eastern border	+	The number of the state highway that runs from Benson to Bisbee	−

$$\underline{\hspace{2cm}} + \underline{\hspace{2cm}} - $$

The number of the state highway that runs east out of the Grand Canyon National Park	+	The number of the Interstate highway that runs east/west through Tucson	=

$$\underline{\hspace{2cm}} + \underline{\hspace{2cm}} = \underline{\hspace{2cm}}$$

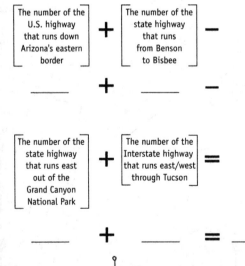

ARkansas

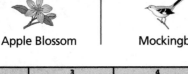

Nickname: The Natural State **Capital:** Little Rock

Pine | Apple Blossom | Mockingbird

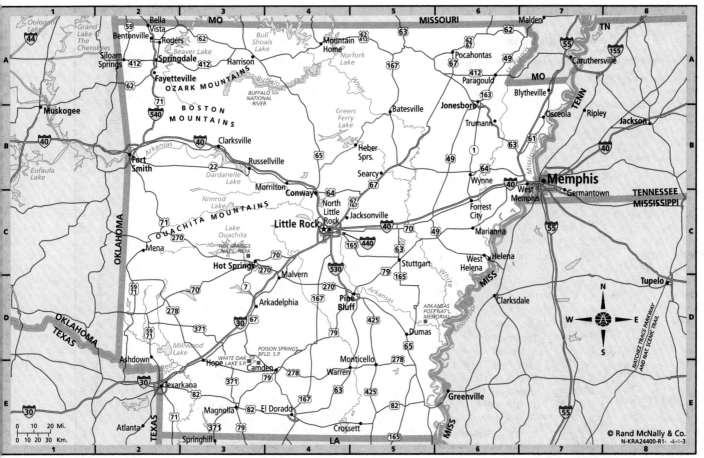

Map of Arkansas © Rand McNally & Co.
N-KRA24400-R1- -4-4-3

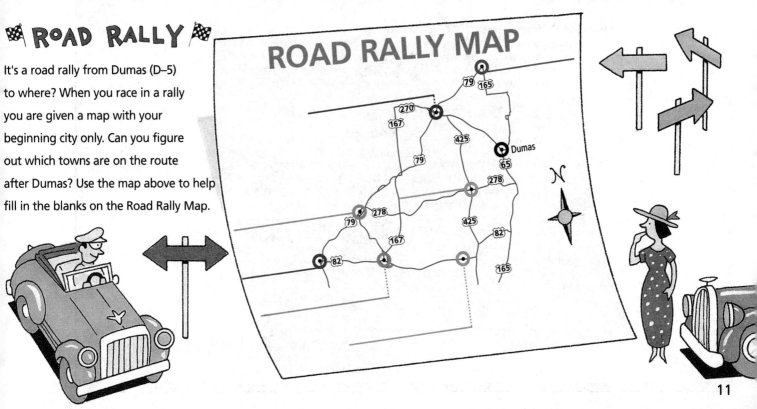

ROAD RALLY

It's a road rally from Dumas (D–5) to where? When you race in a rally you are given a map with your beginning city only. Can you figure out which towns are on the route after Dumas? Use the map above to help fill in the blanks on the Road Rally Map.

ROAD RALLY MAP

11

CAlifornia

Nickname:
The Golden State

Capital:
Sacramento

California Redwood | Golden Poppy | California Valley Quail

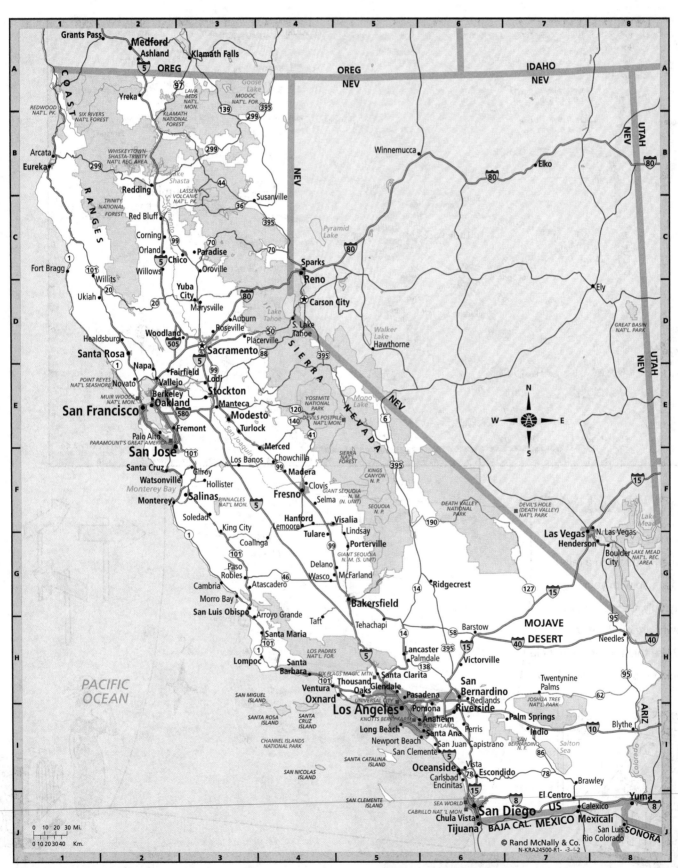

© Rand McNally & Co.
N-KRA24500-R1- -3-4-2

0 10 20 30 Mi.

0 10 20 30 40 Km.

PARK IT HERE

Look on the map of California for the National Parks that are located at the coordinates listed below.

Write the names of the parks in the puzzle. The shaded column will spell out California's state motto, reading from top to bottom.

1. A–1
2. F–5
3. I–7
4. E–4
5. F–5
6. F–6

COlorado

Colorado Blue Spruce	Columbine	Lark Bunting

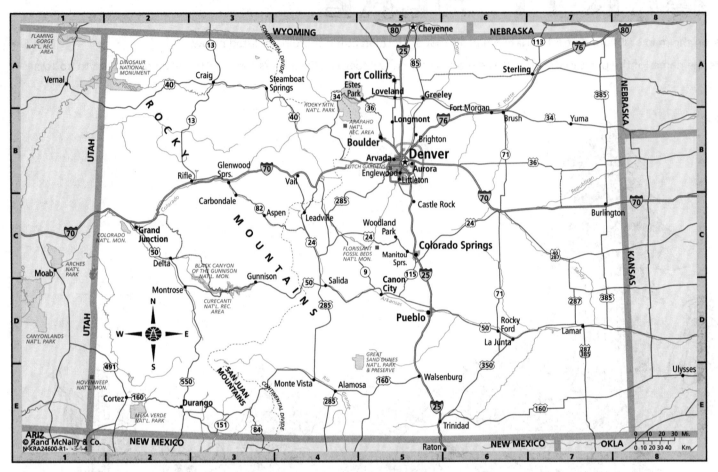

A lot of places in Colorado are named after objects. Look at the pictures below. Can you find the places named after them?

Their coordinates are given in parentheses.

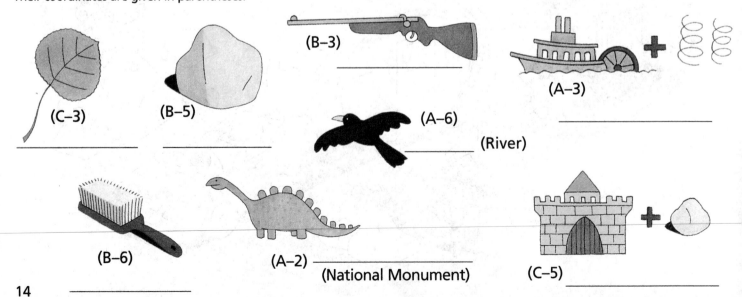

(C–3) _____

(B–5) _____

(B–3) _____

(A–3) _____

(A–6) _____ (River)

(B–6) _____

(A–2) _____ (National Monument)

(C–5) _____

14

ConnecTicut

 White Oak | Mountain Laurel | American Robin

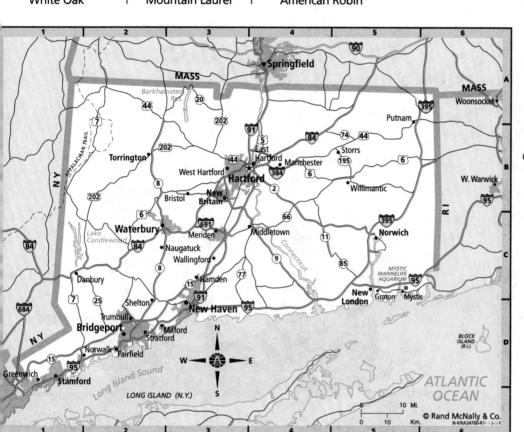

SEA CREATURE

Color the shapes that contain vowels to find out what's at the Mystic Marinelife Aquarium (C–5).

DE|aware

American Holly

Peach Blossom

Blue Hen Chicken

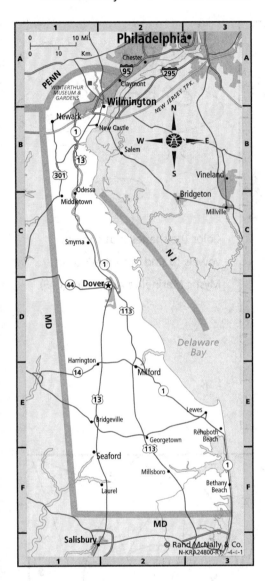

SHIP SHAPE

Delaware is well-known for its maritime history.

Can you spot the correct reflection for this ship?

16

FLORIDA

Nickname:
The Sunshine State

Capital:
Tallahassee

 Sabal Palm

 Orange Blossom

Mockingbird

SIT FOR A SPELL

The Florida beach below shows objects that can be grouped into pairs in which the letters of one thing can be rearranged to spell another. For example, HORSE and SHORE are a pair because they contain the same letters. Rearrange the letters in the words given to make other pairs.

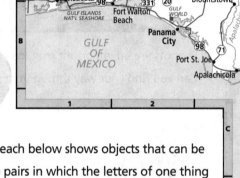

HORSE ___SHORE___	MELON _____
OCEAN _____	TEN _____
PALM _____	SHOE _____
PEARS _____	BEARD _____

GeorgiA

Nickname:
The Peach State

Capital:
Atlanta

| Live Oak | Cherokee Rose | Brown Thrasher |

Peanuts are an important crop in Georgia.

Can you find your way through the peanut maze?

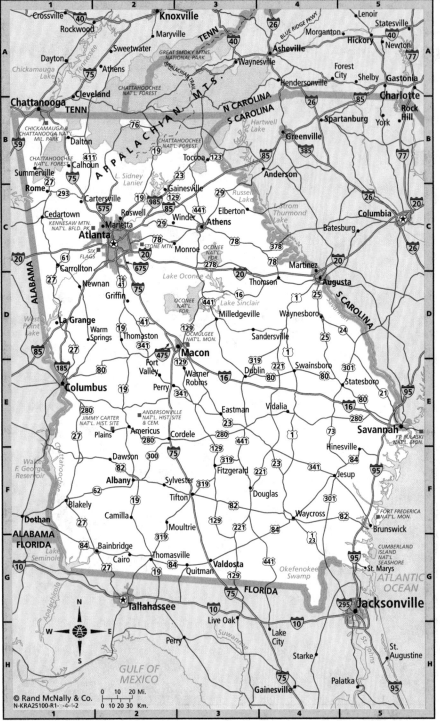

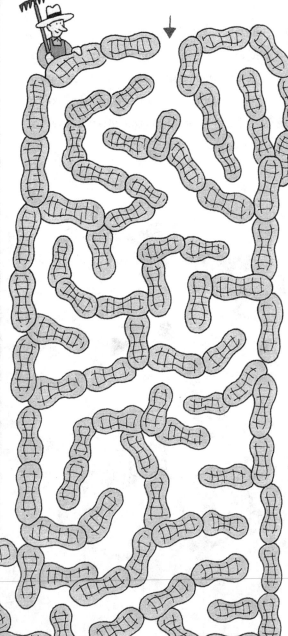

© Rand McNally & Co.
N-KRA25100-R1-·-4-2

0   10   20 Mi.
0 10 20 30 Km.

Hawaii

Nickname:
The Aloha State

Capital:
Honolulu

Kukui (Candlenut) | Yellow Hibiscus | Nene (Hawaiian Goose)

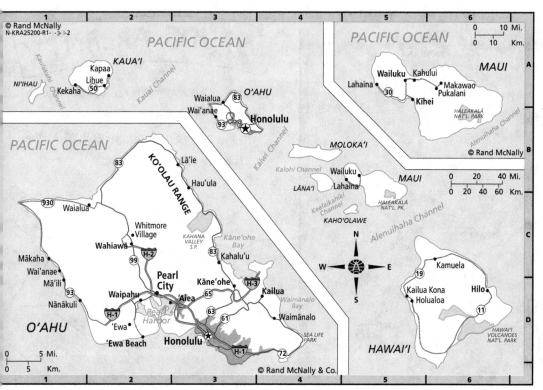

Connect the dots to find out what Kilauea is. Kilauea is in the National Park at coordinate D–6.

19

IDaho

Western White Pine

Syringa (Mock Orange)

Mountain Bluebird

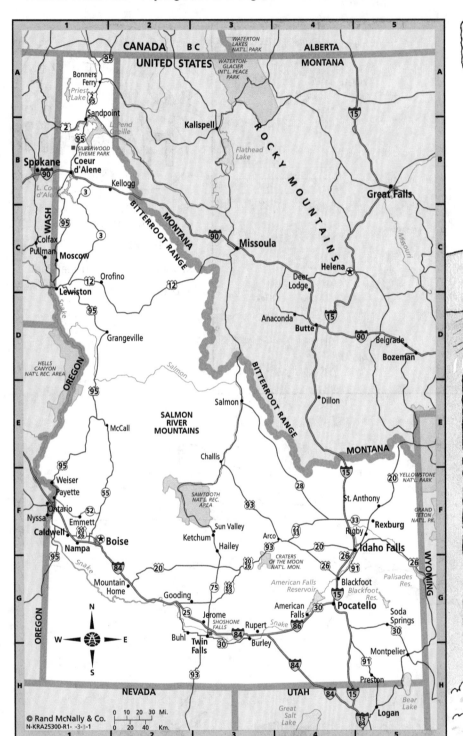

SPUDS APLENTY

Idaho is known for its famous potatoes. Find 5 potatoes and 5 french fries hidden in this picture of Shoshone Falls (G-3), the "Niagara Falls of the West."

© Rand McNally & Co.
N-KRA25300-R1- -3-3-1

ILLinois

Nickname: Land of Lincoln

Capital: Springfield

| White Oak | Native Violet | Cardinal |

ollow the directions for a tour of Illinois. Write the
ames of the cities you visit as you go. If you need a
ttle help, look for the clues in the illustrations below.

_____

A place to say, *"Bonjour"* (E–5)

_____

A place for Santa Claus and Abraham Lincoln (D–2)

_____

A place to have lunch (B–4)

_____

A place to avoid (B–3)

_____

A place to have an average time (C–4)

_____

A place where a poor speller could celebrate (D–4)

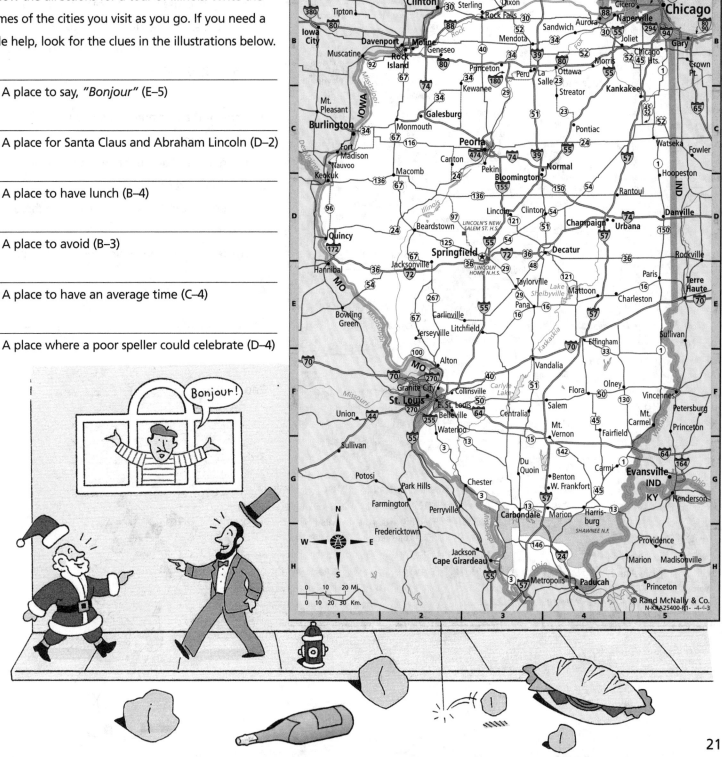

21

INdiana

 Tulip Tree | Peony | Cardinal

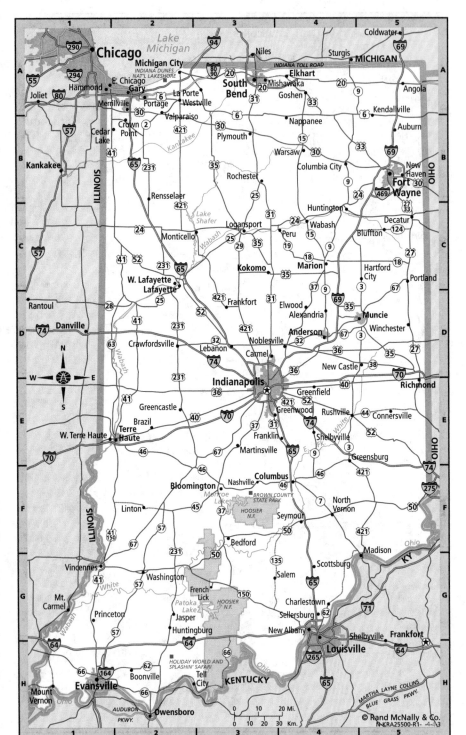

A DAY AT THE RACES

In the Indy 500 car race it can be hard to tell who is winning because some cars can be laps ahead of the others. Use the clues below to figure out which number car is winning and which cars are coming in 2nd and 3rd.

1. None of the odd numbered cars finished in the top three.
2. The gray car didn't finish in the top three.
3. The orange car did win.
4. The brown car didn't finish in the top three either.
5. The red car came in behind the orange car.

1st _____

2nd _____

3rd _____

IOWA

Nickname: The Hawkeye State

Capital: Des Moines

Oak	Wild Rose	Eastern Goldfinch

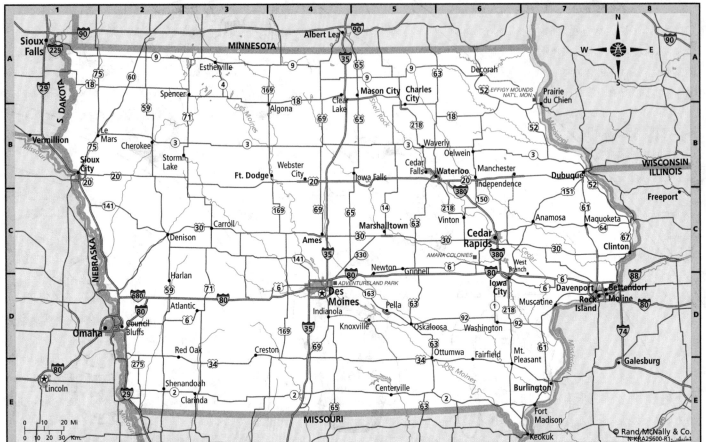

© Rand McNally & Co.

N-KRA25600-R1

FARM JUMBLE

The names of 7 farm animals are mixed up below.

Unscramble them and write the correct names in the boxes.

When you're done, the shaded letters, reading from top to bottom, will spell out the name of something that is made in Iowa.

More of this product is made in Sioux City than in any other place in the world!

1. GIP

2. TROOSER

3. HEEPS

4. CWO

5. TOGA

6. RHOSE

7. NECKHIC

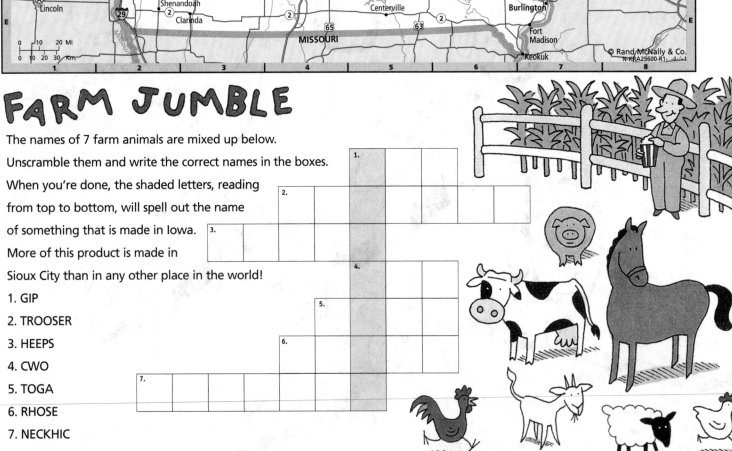

24

KanSas

Cottonwood	Native Sunflower	Western Meadowlark

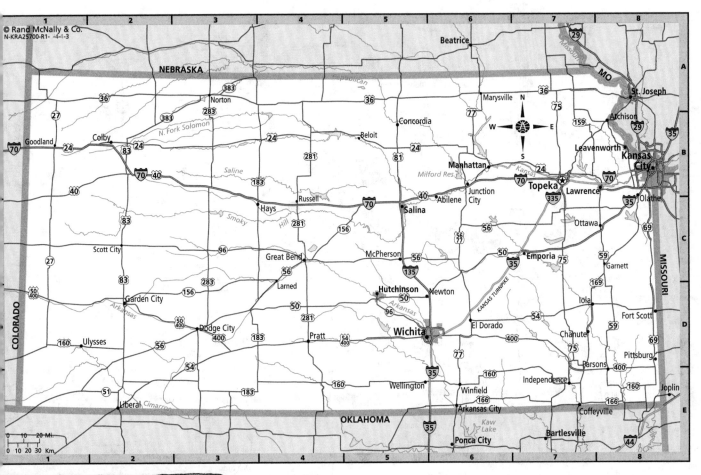

© Rand McNally & Co.
N-KRA25700-R1- -4-1-3

OLD WEST?

Dodge City, Kansas, was a famous town in the Old West.

Circle what doesn't belong in this Old West scene.

KentuckY

Nickname:
The Bluegrass State

Capital:
Frankfort

 Tulip Poplar | Goldenrod | Cardinal

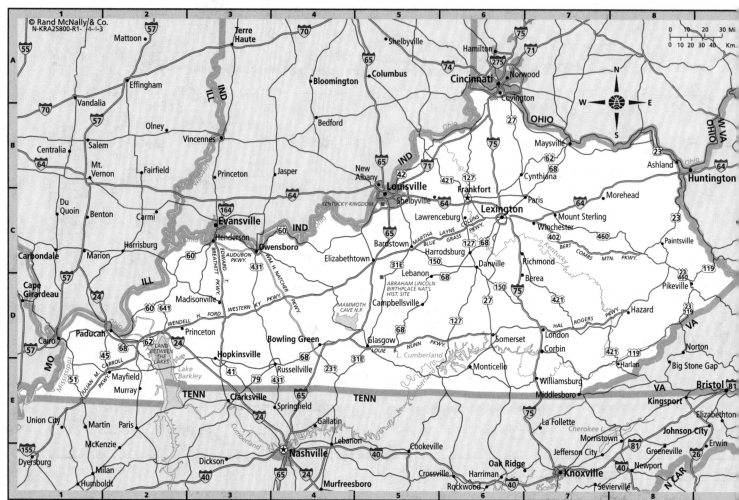

Boy oh Boy!

The name "Ken" can be found in the first three letters of Kentucky.

How many boys' names can you find hidden in the cities on the map of Kentucky?

Hint: All of the names do not occur at the beginning.

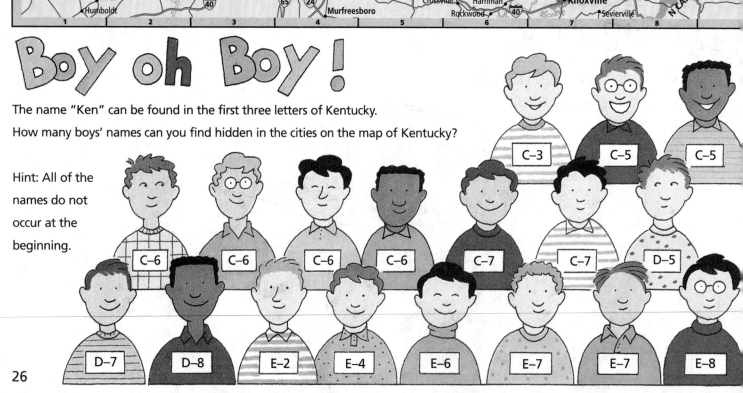

C–3   C–5   C–5

C–6   C–6   C–6   C–6   C–7   C–7   D–5

D–7   D–8   E–2   E–4   E–6   E–7   E–7   E–8

LouisiAna

Nickname:
The Pelican State

Capital:
Baton Rouge

Bald Cypress | Magnolia | Eastern Brown Pelican

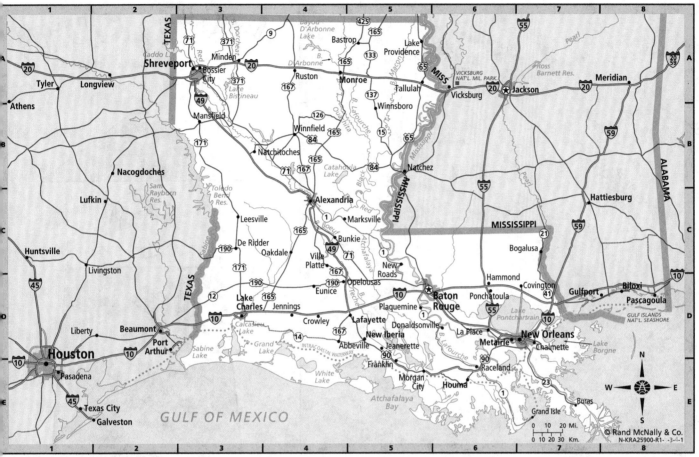

© Rand McNally & Co.
N-KRA25900-R1- -3-4-1

Can you fit the names of these Louisiana rivers, bayous, and lakes into the grid? One of the rivers is in the puzzle to get you started. Hint: Counting the number of letters in the words and using the color code will help.

RIVERS: Mississippi, Red, Ouachita, Sabine, Pearl, Atchafalaya, Black

BAYOUS: Teche, Lafourche, Macon, Boeuf, Dorcheat, D'Arbonne

LAKES: Pontchartrain, Calcasieu, White, Borgne, Caddo, Bistineau, Toledo Bend Reservoir, Grand, Catahoula

27

MainE

Nickname: **The Pine Tree State**   Capital: **Augusta**

 White Pine   White Pine Cone & Tassel   Chickadee

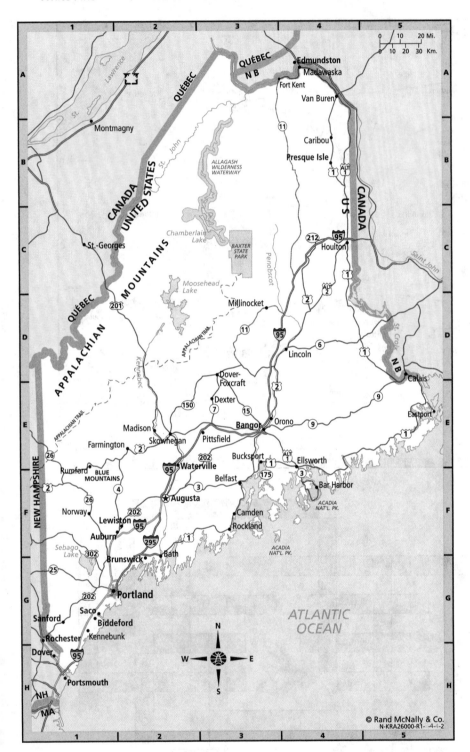

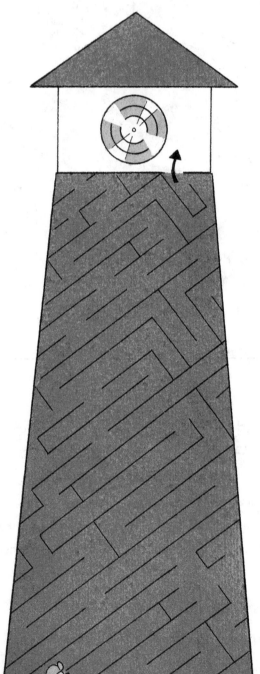

LIGHTS OUT!

Help the lighthouse keeper get to the top to warn the ships.

Maryland

Nickname: The Old Line State **Capital:** Annapolis

 White Oak | Black-eyed Susan | Baltimore Oriole

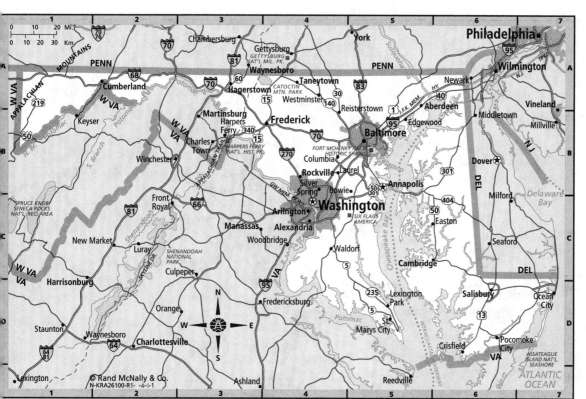

Francis Scott Key wrote the National Anthem in Maryland during the Battle of Baltimore in the War of 1812. Solve the code to find out where he was when he wrote these famous words.

1. Oh! Say can you see, by the dawn's early light,
2. what so proudly we hailed at the twilight's last gleaming?
3. Whose broad stripes and bright stars through the perilous fight,
4. o'er the ramparts we watched were so gallantly streaming?
5. And the rocket's red glare,
6. the bombs bursting in air
7. gave proof through the night
8. that our flag was still there.
9. Oh! Say does that star spangled banner yet wave
10. o'er the land of the free and the home of the brave?

Use the example at the right to understand the code.
The letter G is in line number 1, word number 10, and letter number 3.

G
line   1
word   10
letter   3

H

| 9 1 2 | 7 4 3 | | 8 4 1 | 2 1 3 | 3 6 1 | | 5 1 1 | | 2 3 1 | 4 3 1 | 4 9 7 | 2 8 9 | 4 1 1 | 7 5 1 | 5 5 5 | 5 4 1 |

| 10 9 2 | 10 3 3 | | 8 3 3 | | 9 7 1 | 1 9 3 | 3 3 4 | 4 3 7 | 6 4 1 | 9 2 1 | 7 3 2 | | 2 2 1 | 3 10 4 | 4 9 7 | 7 2 1 |

MAssachusetts

Nickname:
The Bay State

Capital:
Boston

 American Elm

 Mayflower

 Black-capped Chickadee

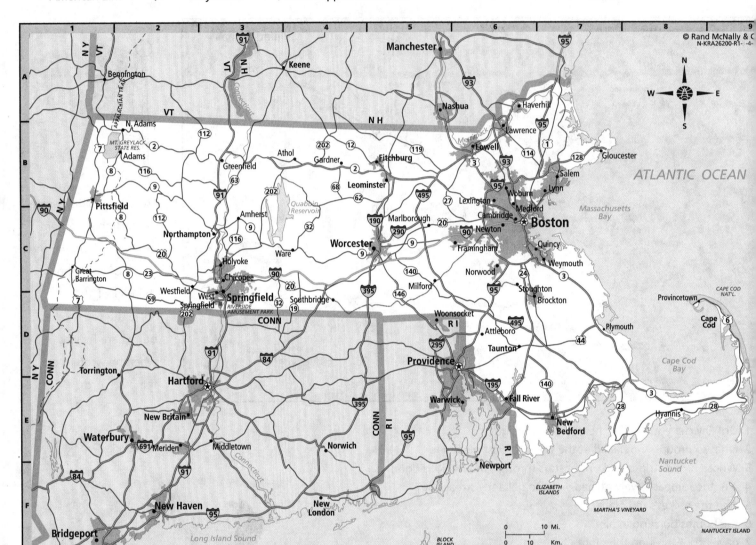

BAY STATERS

Many famous people were born and lived in Massachusetts. Fifteen of them are hidden in the word search on the next page. Only the last names are hidden.

(JOHN) ADAMS	(W.E.B.) DUBOIS	(WINSLOW) HOMER
(LOUISA MAY) ALCOTT	(RALPH WALDO) EMERSON	(JOHN F.) KENNEDY
(SUSAN B.) ANTHONY	(BENJAMIN) FRANKLIN	(EDGAR ALLAN) POE
(CLARA) BARTON	(JOHN) HANCOCK	(PAUL) REVERE
(EMILY) DICKINSON	(OLIVER WENDELL) HOLMES	(NORMAN) ROCKWELL

A D R L P O E
E X I H O L M E S
F A N C D E C E R E
G R R K A H M K R A
M B A I R E E E W H
L S L N R E V H A E N
K E I S K E M N N O L A
N E O O R L C O T R L L
N N N B O I R H C Y
D N C U A N O A
V K E B D T N I D
T H O D T R Y E A
A D A M S Y U

Nickname:
The Wolverine State

Capital:
Lansing

White Pine | Apple Blossom | Robin

Quality Control

You are the inspector on this line of new cars in Detroit, the motor city. Do you see any that look different from the standard? Circle the differences.

STANDARD

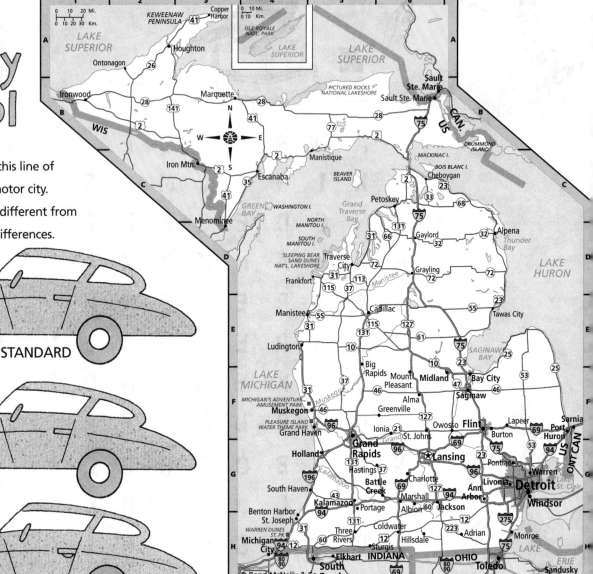

MiNNeSota

Norway Pine | Pink-and-white Lady's Slipper | Common Loon

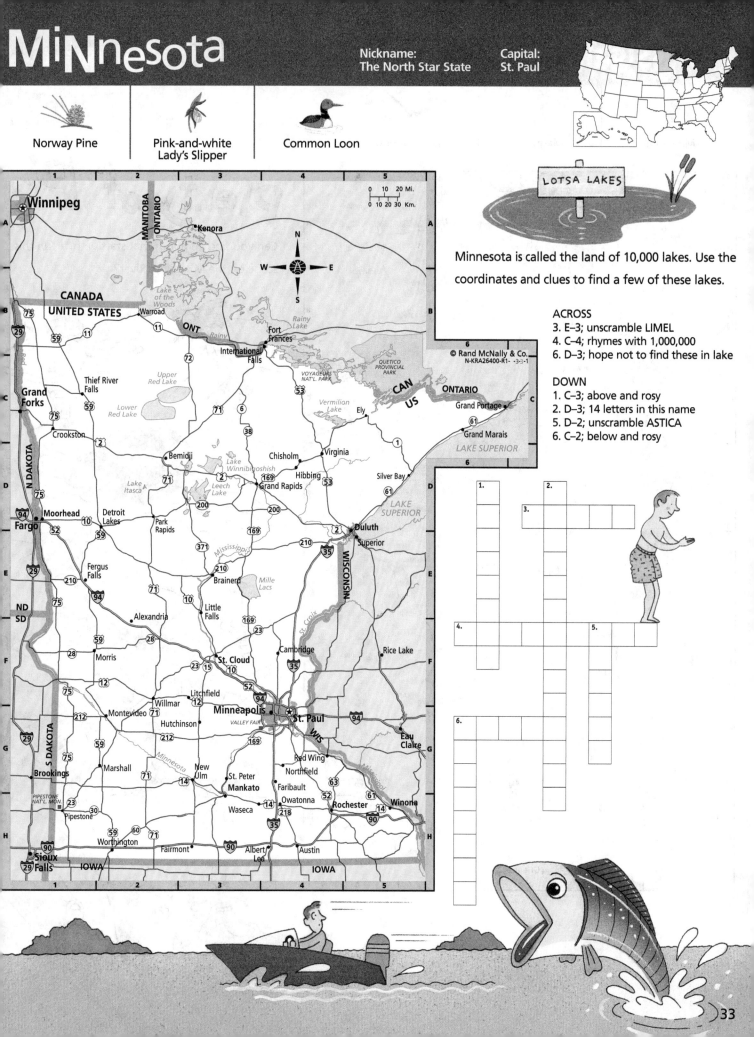

LOTSA LAKES

Minnesota is called the land of 10,000 lakes. Use the coordinates and clues to find a few of these lakes.

ACROSS
3. E–3; unscramble LIMEL
4. C–4; rhymes with 1,000,000
6. D–3; hope not to find these in lake

DOWN
1. C–3; above and rosy
2. D–3; 14 letters in this name
5. D–2; unscramble ASTICA
6. C–2; below and rosy

33

Mississippi

Magnolia

Magnolia

Mockingbird

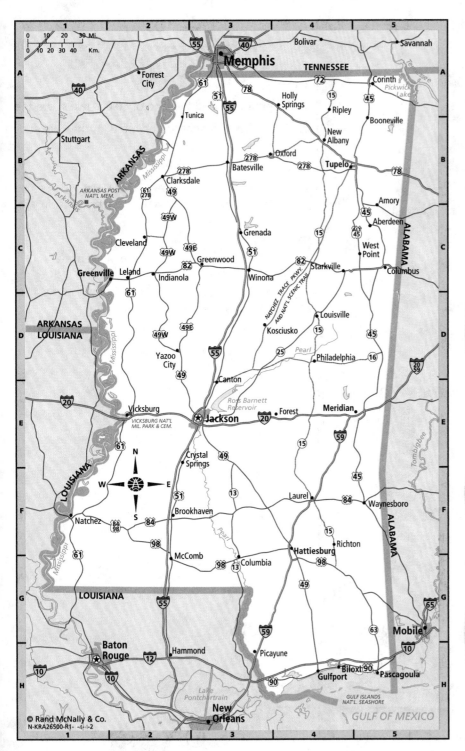

Plenty of P's

Can you find 20 things that start with "P" in this scene on the Mississippi River?

34

Missouri

Nickname:
The Show Me State

Capital:
Jefferson City

 Flowering Dogwood | Hawthorn Blossom | Bluebird

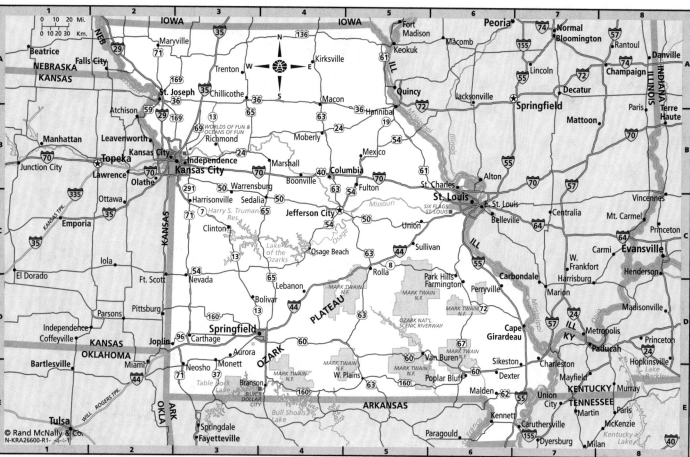

BORDER PATROL

Eight states share borders with Missouri. Can you fit the names of the bordering states into the puzzle?

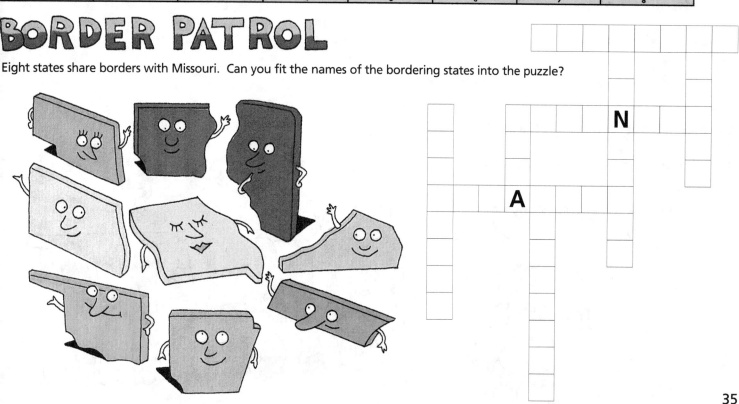

35

MonTana

Ponderosa Pine

Bitterroot

Western Meadowlark

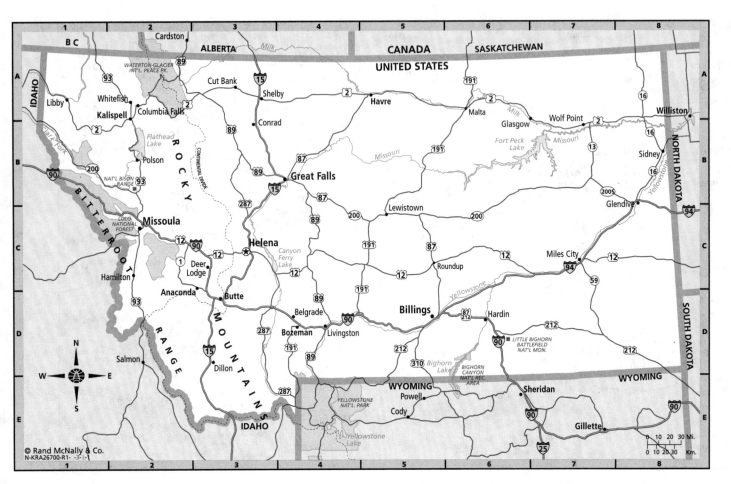

© Rand McNally & Co.
N-KRA26700-R1- -3-3-

SNOWBOARD SHUFFLE

After a morning of boarding at Big Sky, this snowboarder went in for lunch.

When he came out, he couldn't remember where he put his snowboard.

Using the clues that he recalls, help him find his board.

1. His snowboard isn't next to a pair of skis.

2. His snowboard is not blue.

3. His snowboard is next to a blue snowboard.

36

NEbraska

 Cottonwood

 Goldenrod

 Western Meadowlark

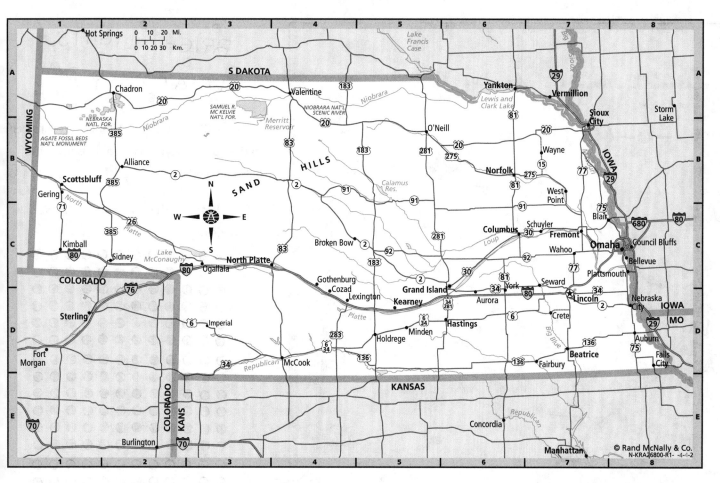

Thrown for a Loop

The cowboy tradition is alive and kicking in Nebraska. Here, a few cowboys have been practicing their roping tricks. Some of the ropes lying on the ground will form knots when both ends are pulled. Can you tell which ones?

NeVada

Nickname:
The Silver State

Capital:
Carson City

| Single-leaf Piñon | Sagebrush | Mountain Bluebird |

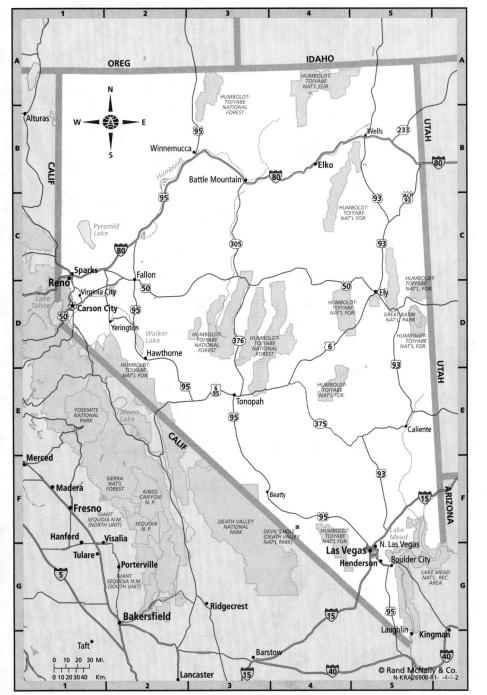

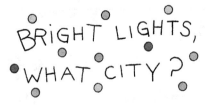

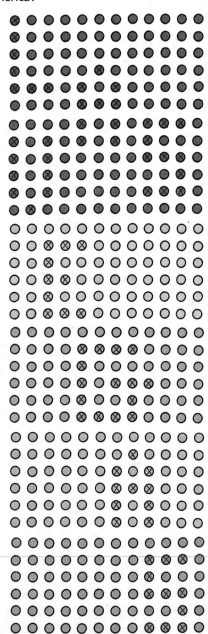

BRIGHT LIGHTS,
WHAT CITY?

Hidden within the colorful lights is the answer to the riddle. All you have to do is fill in the bulbs marked with an "X."

Riddle: What city has the highest electric bills in America?

New Hampshire

Nickname:
The Granite State

Capital:
Concord

White Birch

Purple Lilac

Purple Finch

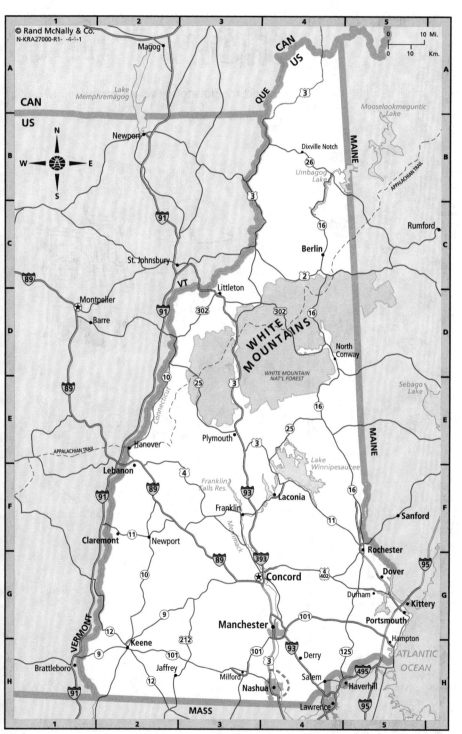

UNDER A SPELL

How many things can you find in the scene below that can only be spelled using letters found in the words NEW HAMPSHIRE?

NEW JERSEY

Nickname:
The Garden State

Capital:
Trenton

 Red Oak

 Purple Violet

Eastern Goldfinch

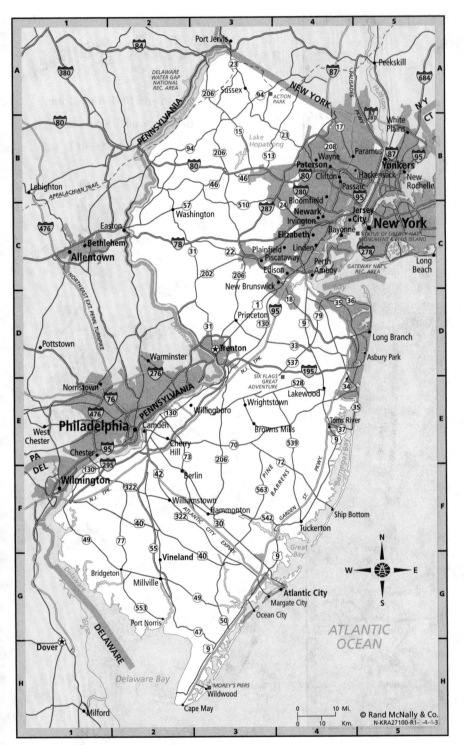

© Rand McNally & Co.
N-KRA27100-R1- 4-4-3

SHORE THINGS

Connect the dots to see what's on this New Jersey beach.

New Mexico

Nickname: Land of Enchantment

Capital: Santa Fe

 Piñon Pine

 Yucca

Roadrunner

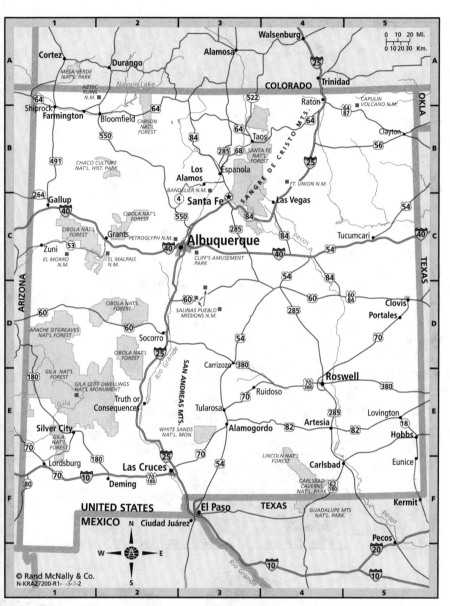

HOT TIME!

The Hot Air Balloon Festival in Albuquerque is the most photographed event of its kind in the world! New Mexico is famous for another hot thing—its Southwestern food. Can you find the 10 chili peppers hiding in this scene?

New York

Sugar Maple

Rose

Red-breasted Bluebird

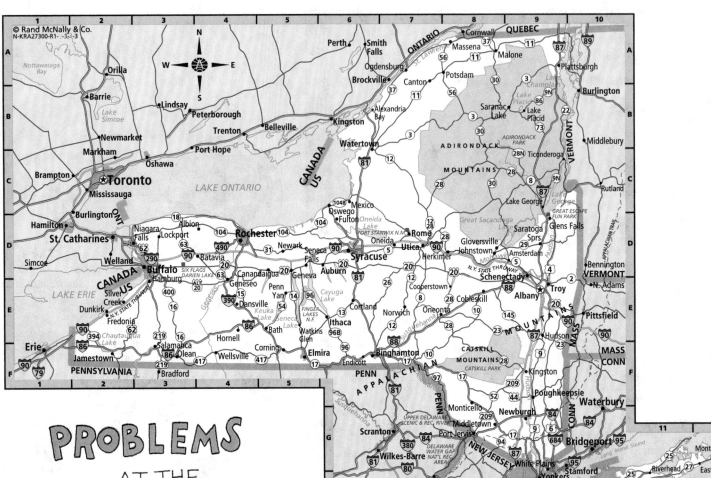

PROBLEMS AT THE PARK

The state of New York has many beautiful parks,

but there seems to be something strange going on in this one.

Can you spot 10 things wrong in the park?

North Carolina

Nickname: The Tar Heel State

Capital: Raleigh

Long Leaf Pine

Dogwood

Cardinal

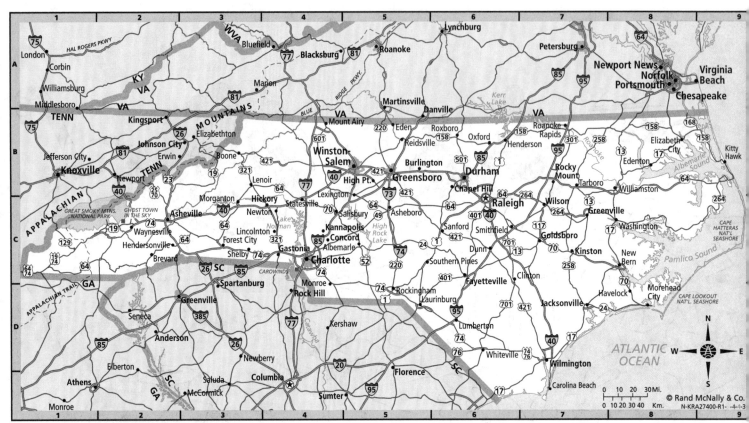

First in Flight

The beach community of Kitty Hawk (B–9) was the site of the Wright brothers' first airplane flight. Try to find all the things that start with "F" in this beach scene.

44

North Dakota

Nickname:
The Peace Garden State

Capital:
Bismarck

American Elm

Wild Prairie Rose

Western Meadowlark

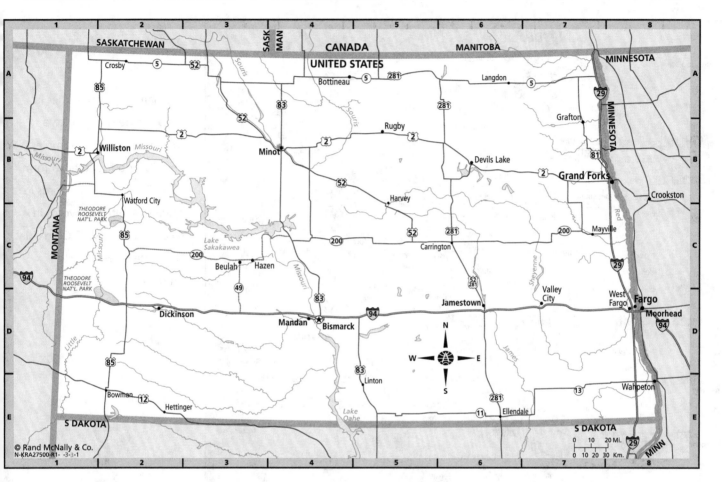

Secret Cities

Figure out the names of 6 North Dakota cities using the word puzzles below.

①  + person =

_____

② rug + bee =

_____

③ bear GRRR + and + fork =

④ foxfox + cake − C + L =

_____

_____

⑤ V +  + city =

⑥ car + ing + ton =

_____

_____

45

OHio

Buckeye

Scarlet Carnation

Cardinal

The names of many cities in Ohio can be split into two smaller words. For example, DAY and TON go together to form DAYTON. Match the words in column A with the words in column B to spell 12 Ohio cities. All of the cities are listed on the map.

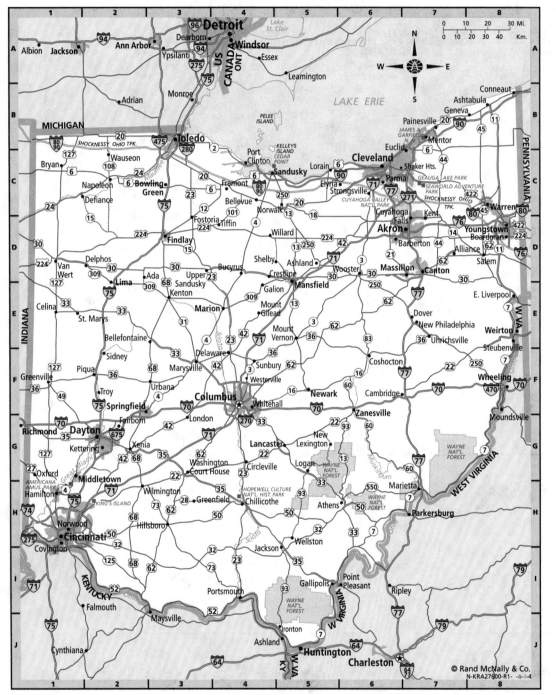

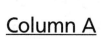

<u>Column A</u>	<u>Column B</u>
FIND	LAND
NEW	MOUTH
ASH	FIELD
CAN	TOWN
WHITE	ARK
SPRING	TON
LOG	BORN
AT	AN
PORTS	FORD
OX	LAY
FAIR	HALL
MIDDLE	HENS

OKlahoma

Redbud

Mistletoe

Scissor-tailed Flycatcher

© Rand McNally & Co.
N-KRA27700-R1- -4-4-2

SCRAMBLED CiTiES

Unscramble the names of these Oklahoma towns and you'll be OK!

DINE (A–5) _____

BILEAD (D–8) _____

LOWTAN (C–5) _____

WLASSAIL (B–8) _____

LEEKOMUG (B–7) _____

MOUNGY (A–2)_____

USALT (B–7) _____

AMIMI (A–8) _____

SHEENWA (C–6) _____

TALLIWERTS (B–6)_____

48

ORegon

Nickname:
The Beaver State

Capital:
Salem

Douglas Fir | Oregon Grape | Western Meadowlark

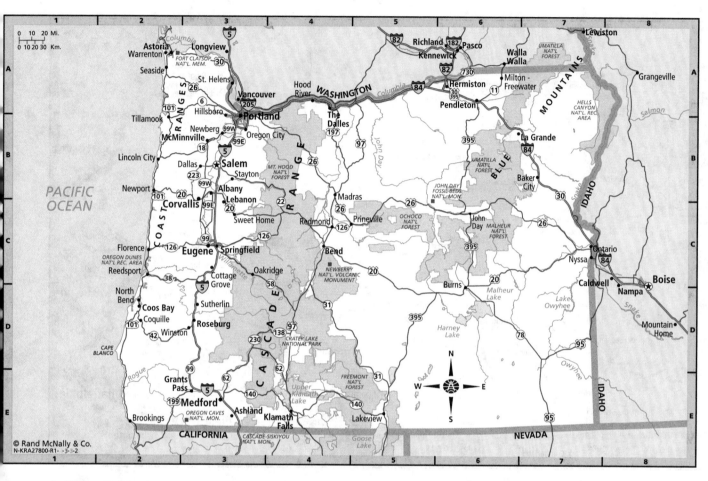

DIVE IN

These two tide pools on the Oregon coast are almost exactly alike.

Can you spot the differences between them?

PennsylvAnia

Nickname: The Keystone State
Capital: Harrisburg

Hemlock

Mountain Laurel

Ruffed Grouse

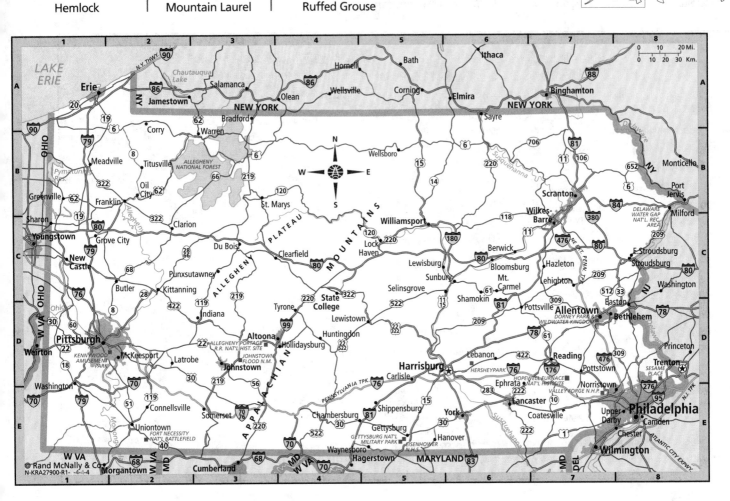

Two of a kind

Two of the squares in this Pennsylvania Dutch quilt are exactly the same. Can you find them?

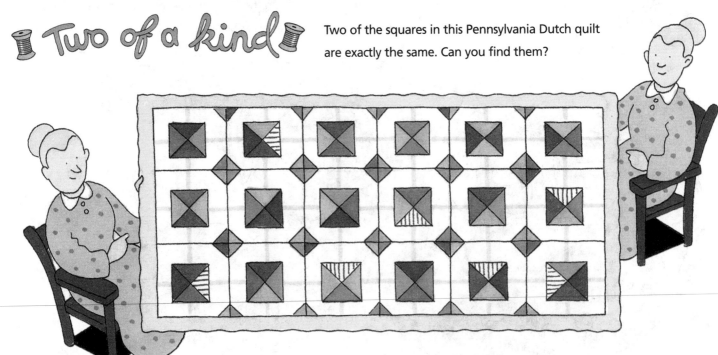

Rhode Island

Nickname: The Ocean State **Capital:** Providence

 Red Maple | Violet | Rhode Island Red

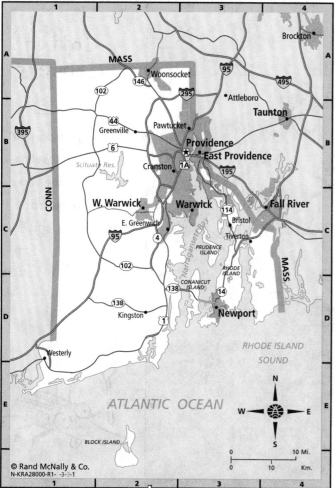

IN THE RED

People in Rhode Island must like the color red. Their state bird is the Rhode Island Red and their state tree is the Red Maple. Use the clues below to identify words that have RED in them?

1. Stop signal _____

2. Tall California tree_____

3. Colors of the U.S. flag_____

4. Become very angry_____

5. Story about a girl, her grandmother, and a wolf_____

_____

6. Walking surface for movie stars_____

7. Carrot top_____

South Carolina

Nickname: The Palmetto State

Capital: Columbia

Palmetto

Carolina Jessamine

Carolina Wren

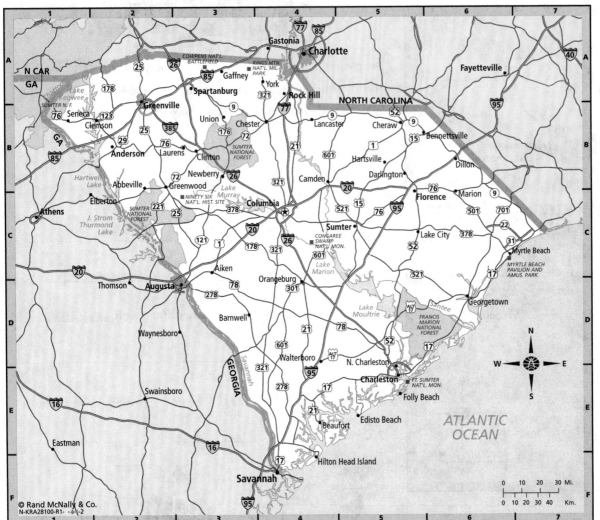

Cotton Critters

Cotton is an important crop in South Carolina. Can you find the pesky boll weevils hidden in the cotton plants? Cross them out before they damage the cotton.

South Dakota

 Black Hills Spruce

 Pasque Flower

Chinese Ring-necked Pheasant

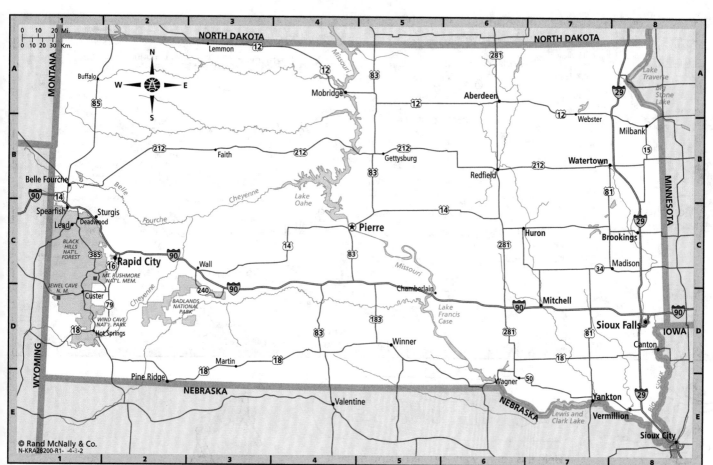

© Rand McNally & Co.
N-KRA28200-R1- -4-3-2

The pictures below show the steps in making a sweater—starting with shearing a sheep for wool. However, the pictures are not in the right order. If you write the letters in the corner of the pictures in the order in which they should be placed, the letters will complete a fact about South Dakota.

In South Dakota, there are twice as many sheep as _____ _____ _____ _____ _____ _____ .

53

TeNNeSSee

Tulip Poplar

Iris

Mockingbird

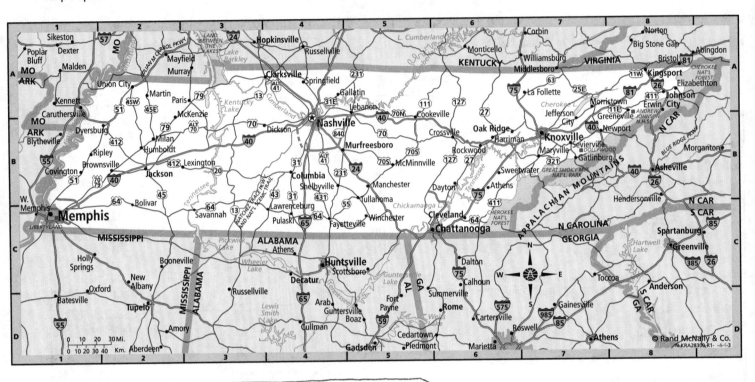

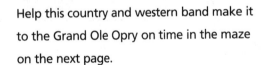

TUNE TIME

Help this country and western band make it
to the Grand Ole Opry on time in the maze
on the next page.

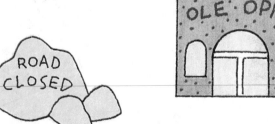

ROAD
CLOSED

GRAND
OLE OPRY

ROAD CLOSED

STOP

GRAND OLE OPRY

TeXas

Pecan

Bluebonnet

Mockingbird

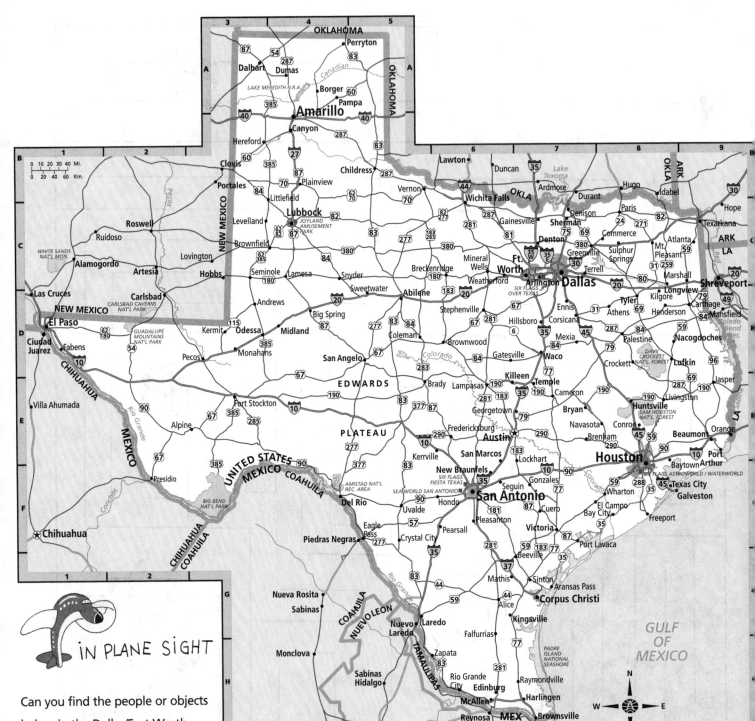

OKLAHOMA

Perryton

Dalhart   Dumas

Canadian

LAKE MEREDITH N.R.A.

Borger

Pampa

Amarillo

Canyon

Hereford

Clovis

Plainview

Portales

Littlefield

Lubbock
JOYLAND
AMUSEMENT
PARK

Levelland

Brownfield

Roswell

Ruidoso

Lovington

Seminole

Alamogordo

Artesia

Hobbs

Lamesa

Snyder

Las Cruces

Carlsbad
CARLSBAD CAVERNS
NAT'L PARK

El Paso

NEW MEXICO

Andrews

Sweetwater

Abilene

Ciudad
Juarez   Fabens

GUADALUPE
MOUNTAINS
NAT'L PARK

Kermit   Odessa   Midland

Big Spring

CHIHUAHUA

Pecos   Monahans

San Angelo

Villa Ahumada

Fort Stockton

EDWARDS

Brady

MEXICO

Alpine

PLATEAU

Chihuahua

Presidio

BIG BEND
NAT'L PARK

Conchos

UNITED STATES
MEXICO   COAHUILA

AMISTAD NAT'L
REC. AREA

Del Rio

Uvalde

Eagle
Pass

Piedras Negras

Crystal City

Pearsall

OKLAHOMA

Lawton

Duncan

Ardmore

Hugo

Idabel

Wichita Falls

OKLA

Durant

Paris

Texarkana

Hope

ARK

LA

Vernon

Gainesville

Sherman

Denison

Commerce

Atlanta

Denton

Greenville

Mt.
Pleasant

Marshall

Shreveport

Breckenridge

Mineral
Wells

Ft.
Worth

Arlington Dallas

Terrell

SIX FLAGS
OVER TEXAS

Longview

Kilgore

Carthage

Weatherford

Tyler

Henderson

Mansfield

Stephenville

Athens

Hillsboro

Corsicana

Palestine

Nacogdoches

Coleman

Brownwood

Gatesville

Waco

Mexia

Crockett

DAVY
CROCKETT
NAT'L FOREST

Lufkin

Jasper

Colorado

Killeen

Temple

Lampasas

Cameron

Livingston

Georgetown

Bryan

Huntsville
SAM HOUSTON
NAT'L FOREST

Fredericksburg

Navasota

Conroe

Beaumont

Orange

Kerrville

Austin

Brenham

New Braunfels

SIX FLAGS
FIESTA TEXAS

San Marcos

Lockhart

Houston

Baytown

Port
Arthur

SEA WORLD SAN ANTONIO

Seguin

Gonzales

SIX FLAGS ASTROWORLD / WATERWORLD

Texas City

San Antonio

Hondo

Cuero

Wharton

Galveston

Pleasanton

Victoria

El Campo

Bay City

Freeport

Port Lavaca

Beeville

Mathis

Sinton

Aransas Pass

Nueva Rosita

Corpus Christi

Sabinas

Alice

COAHUILA

NUEVO LEON

Nuevo
Laredo

Laredo

Kingsville

GULF
OF
MEXICO

Monclova

Falfurrias

TAMAULIPAS

Zapata

PADRE
ISLAND
NATIONAL
SEASHORE

Sabinas
Hidalgo

Rio Grande
City

Edinburg

Raymondville

McAllen

Harlingen

Reynosa   MEX

Monterrey

Brownsville

Saltillo

Matamoros

Rio Grande

B
0 10 20 30 40 Mi.
0 20 40 60 Km.

IN PLANE SIGHT

Can you find the people or objects
below in the Dallas/Fort Worth
airport scene on the next page?

© Rand McNally & Co.
N-KRA28400-R1- -3-4-2

UTah

Nickname:
The Beehive State

Capital:
Salt Lake City

Blue Spruce | Sego Lily | American Seagull

PARK PLACE

Utah is home to many National Parks and Monuments.
Circle the names, listed below the map, in the puzzle.

T	G	R	P	P	H	B	L	S	T	I	Y	T
T	L	I	N	E	S	A	R	C	H	E	S	C
A	E	B	A	O	R	E	Z	Q	R	O	M	H
Z	N	N	T	P	D	I	N	O	S	A	U	R
R	C	O	U	L	E	N	N	B	K	I	R	I
O	A	O	R	E	F	G	S	G	N	T	A	S
L	N	T	A	O	E	X	D	O	Z	B	D	Q
N	Y	F	L	F	G	G	I	L	L	I	B	K
G	O	G	B	E	C	W	N	D	A	W	O	E
L	N	K	R	A	P	S	H	E	C	V	Y	N
A	S	T	I	R	D	O	U	N	H	R	R	D
D	D	A	D	T	E	N	D	S	B	O	C	R
E	T	E	G	H	V	P	L	P	A	I	H	A
N	X	R	E	O	Y	T	S	I	M	I	S	I
S	O	R	S	K	B	R	A	K	N	S	O	V
C	A	P	I	T	O	L	R	E	E	F	G	S
M	G	I	L	K	B	I	I	J	R	I	O	O
A	Q	R	L	E	B	S	H	O	A	O	N	G
O	J	C	R	A	Y	A	D	C	L	N	A	H
C	A	N	Y	O	N	L	A	N	D	S	P	C
T	A	H	H	R	N	I	M	L	A	W	M	I
R	C	A	L	E	X	S	Y	T	L	P	I	N
S	K	A	E	R	B	R	A	D	E	C	T	C

ARCHES   GLEN CANYON

CANYONLANDS   GOLDEN SPIKE

CAPITOL REEF   NATURAL BRIDGES

CEDAR BREAKS   TIMPANOGOS

DINOSAUR   ZION

VermonT

Nickname: The Green Mountain State

Capital: Montpelier

Sugar Maple

Red Clover

Hermit Thrush

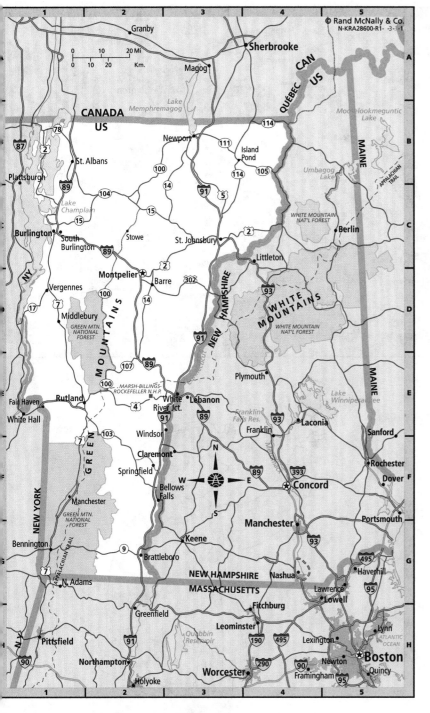

Unbelievable

All of the facts about Vermont below are true…except for one. To find out which one is not true, solve the equation. The value of X will equal the number next to the false statement.

1. Native Americans taught Europeans how to tap maple trees for syrup.

2. Only Alaska and Wyoming have fewer residents than Vermont.

3. Vermont was once its own country, with its own money!

4. Grandma Moses, a Vermont painter, worked until she was 101 years old.

5. Ice cream from Vermont is popular because cows there have a higher cream content in their milk.

X = The number of the false fact

$X = A - B + C$

$A = B + 4$

$B = C + 2$

$C = 1$

VirginiA

Dogwood

Dogwood Blossom

Cardinal

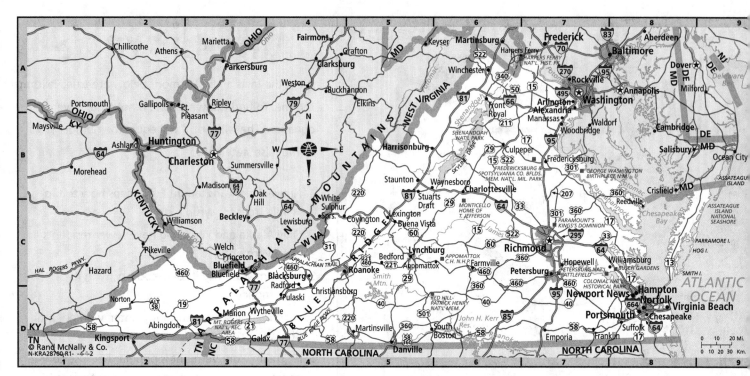

© Rand McNally & Co.
N-KRA28700-R1- -4- -2

This Virginia city was the center of politics and culture in colonial times. Use the clues to find out the name of this city.

1. It's about 50 miles southeast of Richmond.
2. It's about 35 miles northwest of Norfolk.
3. It's at coordinate C-7.

The city is _____.

WAshington

Nickname: The Evergreen State

Capital: Olympia

Western Hemlock

Coast Rhododendron

Willow Goldfinch

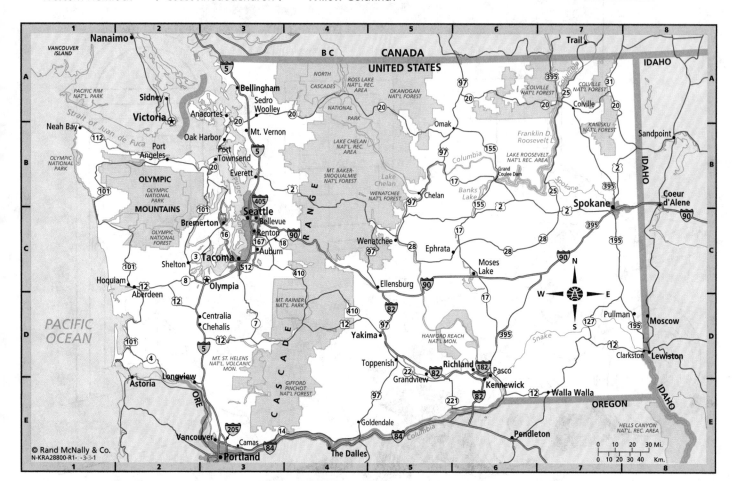

© Rand McNally & Co.
N-KRA28800-R1- -3- -1

Picture Quiz

Write the **last** letters of the objects below in the boxes. When you're finished, the letters will spell out the name of an event that was started in 1909 by Sonora Louise Smart Dodd in Spokane, Washington.

,

____ ____ ____ ____ ____ ____ ____ ____

____ ____ ____

West Virginia

Sugar Maple

Rhododendron

Cardinal

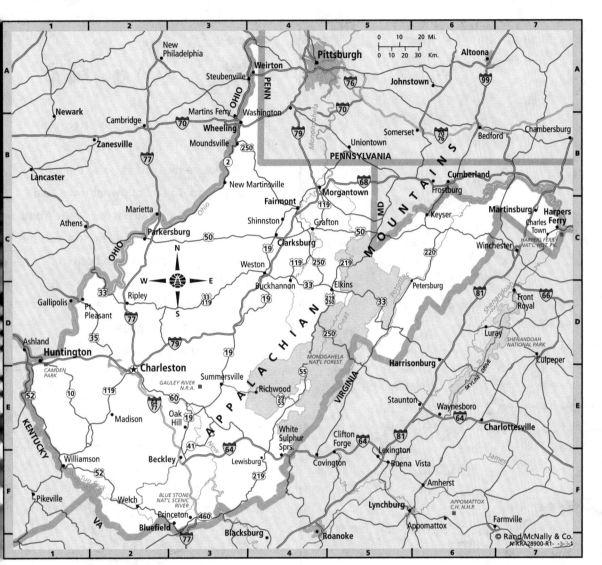

Cross out the words that answer the clues. An interesting fact about West Virginia will be left when you're finished.

CLUES

1. The town directly across the river from Steubenville, Ohio
2. The river that makes up most of the west border
3. The town that is "NOT SEW" scrambled
4. The "dishonest" river
5. The town that is the farthest east
6. The river that joins the Shenandoah River at Harpers Ferry
7. The river that makes up part of the southwestern border
8. The state that borders West Virginia to the southwest
9. The state capital

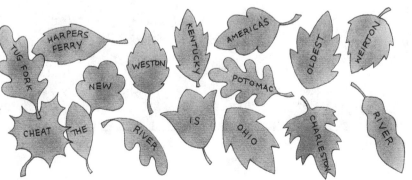

63

WIsconsin

Nickname: The Badger State

Capital: Madison

Sugar Maple | Wood Violet | Robin

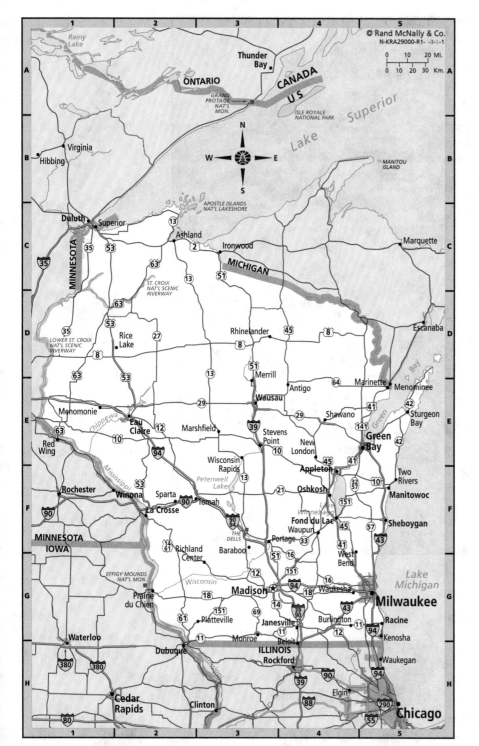

In 1884, five brothers held their first circus with farm animals and jugglers in Wisconsin. Over time, it became the world famous Ringling Brothers Circus. To find out what town held that first event, and now has the Circus World Museum, solve the puzzle below and read the one-letter answers from top to bottom.

1. A letter in BEAR but not in TRAPEZE _____
2. A letter in LAKE and MICHIGAN _____
3. A letter in SPARTA and MERRILL _____
4. A letter in SUGAR and MAPLE _____
5. A letter in BRIE but not AMERICAN _____
6. A letter in HOLSTEIN and COW _____
7. A letter in TRACTOR but not CART _____

WYoming

Cottonwood

Indian Paintbrush

Western Meadowlark

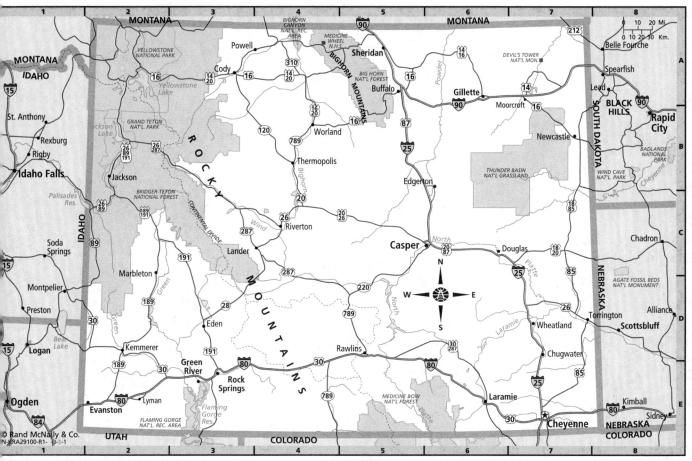

© Rand McNally & Co.
N-KRA29100-R1- B-3-1

Climb to the top! Start at the bottom left and see if you can make it to the top of Devil's Tower (A–7).

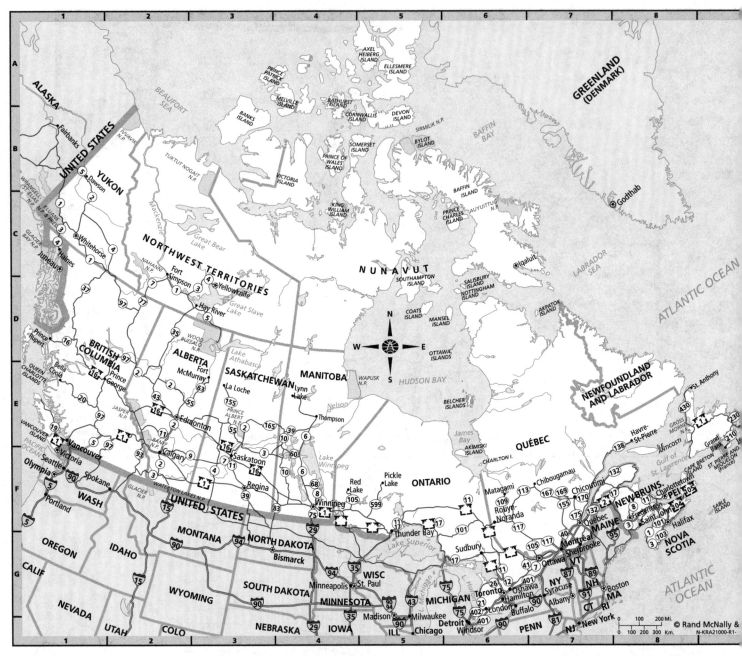

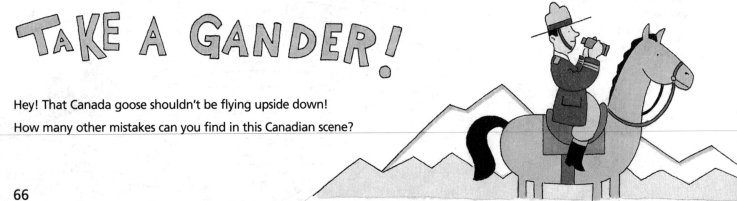

TAKE A GANDER!

Hey! That Canada goose shouldn't be flying upside down!

How many other mistakes can you find in this Canadian scene?

Mexico

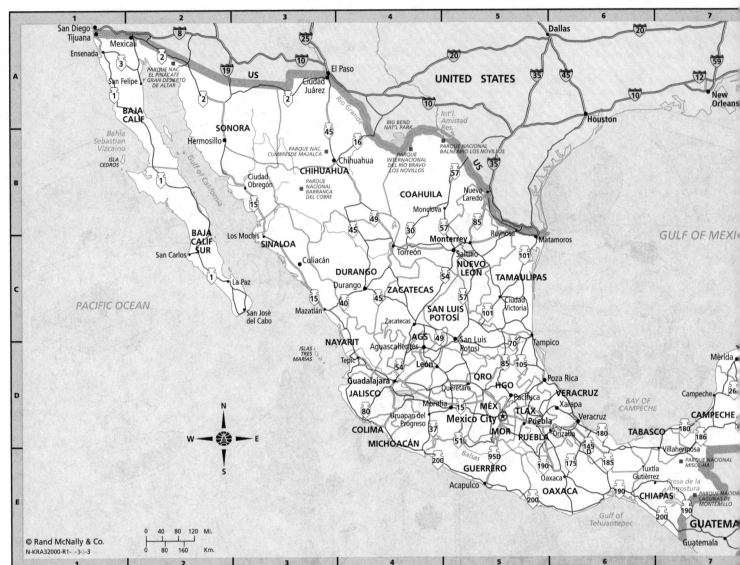

1. This body of water is to the east of Quintana Roo.

2. This city is directly south of San Diego, California.

3. This state on the south of the Bay of Campeche has the same name as a spicy sauce.

4. This food is a flat bread made from corn.

5. This river, or *rio*, forms much of the border between Mexico and the U.S.

6. This cliff-diving location is the southernmost point on 95D.

7. This city's name is a combination of Mexico and California.

8. This state in northern Mexico shares its name with a breed of dogs.

9. This body of water lies west of the Baja Peninsula.

10. This country lies east of Chiapas.

11. As you take 45 north, the last city you go through before leaving Mexico is _____.

12. This city is directly across the border to the north of question #11.

13. This country is south of Quintana Roo.

14. This "little beautiful" city is a major one in the state of Sonora.

SOUTH of the BORDER

Cross out the words in the puzzle that answer the questions on the opposite page.

An interesting fact about Mexico will be left when you're finished. Read it from top to bottom.

MEXICANS

TIJUANA
BELIZE
WERE
ACAPULCO
EL PASO
KNOWN
CIUDAD JUAREZ
THE
MEN
MEXICALI
OF
HERMOSILLO
TABASCO

RIO GRANDE

ONCE

CARIBBEAN SEA

GUATEMALA

CORN

TORTILLA

AS

CHIHUAHUA

PACIFIC OCEAN

License Plate Game

Keep an eye out for license plates from all over the U.S.
Cross off the state when you see its plate.

Alabama	Hawaii	Massachusetts	New Mexico	South Dakota
Alaska	Idaho	Michigan	New York	Tennessee
Arizona	Illinois	Minnesota	North Carolina	Texas
Arkansas	Indiana	Mississippi	North Dakota	Utah
California	Iowa	Missouri	Ohio	Vermont
Colorado	Kansas	Montana	Oklahoma	Virginia
Connecticut	Kentucky	Nebraska	Oregon	Washington
Delaware	Louisiana	Nevada	Pennsylvania	West Virginia
Florida	Maine	New Hampshire	Rhode Island	Wisconsin
Georgia	Maryland	New Jersey	South Carolina	Wyoming

Answers

Using an Atlas

Pages 4–5
Everglades; Florida; Denver; Colorado; Newport Beach; California; Tijuana
The adventure begins with a turn of the page!

United States

Page 7
1. AL; 2. AK; 3. AZ; 4. AR; 5. CA; 6. CO; 7. CT; 8. DE; 9. FL;
10. GA; 11. HI; 12. ID; 13. IL; 14. IN; 15. IA; 16. KS; 17. KY;
18. LA; 19. ME; 20. MD; 21. MA; 22. MI; 23. MN; 24. MS;
25. MO; 26. MT; 27. NE; 28. NV; 29. NH; 30. NJ; 31. NM; 32. NY;
33. NC; 34. ND; 35. OH; 36. OK; 37. OR; 38. PA; 39. RI; 40. SC;
41. SD; 42. TN; 43. TX; 44. UT; 45. VT; 46. VA; 47. WA; 48. WV;
49. WI; 50. WY

ALabama

Page 8
Huntsville, Alabama

AlasKa

Page 9

AriZona

Page 10
How deep?
40 ÷ 10 = 4 Empire State Buildings (up to 5,500 feet deep)
How long?
191 + 80 − 64 + 10 = 217 miles long (Illinois is 218 miles wide)

ARkansas

Page 11
Stuttgart, Pine Bluff, Camden, Magnolia, El Dorado, Crosset, Monticello

CAlifornia

Page 13
1. Redwood; 2. Sequoia; 3. Joshua Tree; 4. Yosemite;
5. Kings Canyon; 6. Death Valley
State Motto: "Eureka!"

COlorado

Page 14
C–3 Aspen; B–5 Boulder; B–3 Rifle; A–3 Steamboat Springs;
B–6 Brush; A–2 Dinosaur National Monument; A–6 Crow River;
C–5 Castle Rock

ConnecTicut

Page 15

(Penguins)

DElaware

Page 16

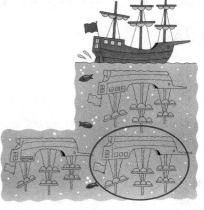

FLorida

Page 17
OCEAN and CANOE; PALM and LAMP; PEARS and SPEAR;
MELON and LEMON; TEN and NET; SHOE and HOSE; BEARD and BREAD

GeorgiA

Page 18

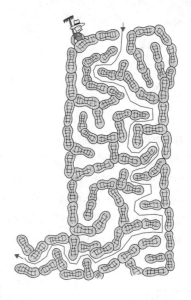

Hawaii

Page 19
Kilauea is an active volcano in Hawaii Volcanoes National Park.

Answers

IDaho
Page 20

ILLinois
Page 21

1. Paris; 2. Beardstown;
3. Sandwich; 4. Rock Falls;
5. Normal; 6. Champaign

INdiana
Page 22

1st – #8 Yellow; 2nd – #2 Orange; 3rd – #10 Red

IowA
Page 24

More popcorn is produced in Sioux City, Iowa, than in any other place in the world.

KanSas
Page 25

KentuckY
Page 26

(C-3) Owensboro; (C-5) Louisville and Shelbyville;
(C-6) Danville, Lawrenceburg, Frankfort, Harrodsburg,
or Lexington; (C-7) Richmond and Winchester;
(D-5) Campbellsville; (D-7) London; (D-8) Pikeville;
(E-2) Murray; (E-4) Russellville; (E-6) Monticello;
(E-7) Williamsburg and Middlesboro;
(E-8) Harlan

LouisiAna
Page 27

IDAHO

MainE
Page 28

MarylanD
Page 29

He was a prisoner on a British ship.

MAssachusetts
Page 31

MIchigan
Page 32

MiNNesota
Page 33

Across: 3. Mille; 4. Vermilion; 6. Leech
Down: 1. Upper Red; 2. Winnibigoshish; 5. Itasca; 6. Lower Red

MiSsiSsippi
Page 34

paddlewheel, post, pier, pirate, patch (eye), parrot, pegleg,
pipe, picnic, plate, paw, person, pants, pig, pony, pineapple,
pillow, palm tree, pail, path, park bench, pepper, park, puddle,
periscope, poodle, paddle, plane, pencil, pelican, parking mete

MissOuri
Page 35

MonTana
Page 36

NEbraska
Page 37

NeVada
Page 38

Las Vegas

New Hampshire
Page 39

ship, ramp, shrimp, wasp, man, pines, hen, map, harp, pear, pie, peas, sheep, saw

New Jersey
Page 40

New Mexico
Page 41

NEW JERSEY

NEW MEXICO

New York
Page 43

mail box, periscope, sail boat on rock, snow boarder, candy cane, chimney on tent, fishing in fire, fire hydrant, dolphin in stream, shoe in tree

North Carolina
Page 44

frog, flashlight, fish, fin (on fish), flamingo, feather, fire or flame, fruit, flower, farmer, fan, flag, flippers, football, fork, foot/feet, face, forehead, fingers, fringe, frisbee (on towel or blanket), four (on t-shirt), fence, funnel, floats, frankfurter

North Dakota
Page 45

1. Bowman; 2. Rugby; 3. Grand Forks; 4. Devils Lake;
5. Valley City; 6. Carrington

OHio
Page 47

Findlay, Newark, Ashland, Canton, Whitehall, Springfield, Logan, Athens, Portsmouth, Oxford, Fairborn, Middletown

OKlahoma
Page 48

dine – Enid (A–5); bilead – Idabel (D–8); lowtan – Lawton (C–5); wlassail – Sallisaw (B–8); leekomug – Okmulgee (B–7); moungy – Guymon (A–2); usalt – Tulsa (B–7); amimi – Miami (A–8); sheenwa – Shawnee (C–6); talliwerts – Stillwater (B–6)

ORegon
Page 49

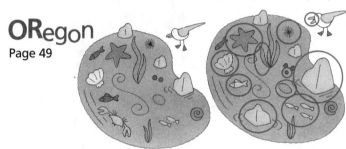

PennsylvAnia
Page 50

Rhode Island
Page 51

1. red light; 2. redwood; 3. red, white, and blue; 4. see red;
5. Little Red Riding Hood; 6. red carpet; 7. redhead

South Carolina
Page 52

Answers

South Dakota
Page 53
The correct order is P, E, O, P, L, E, which spells out PEOPLE

TeNnessee
Page 54

TeXas
Page 57

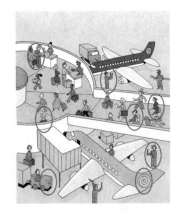

UTah
Page 58

VermonT
Page 59
A = 7; B = 3; C = 1; X = 5
Fact number 5 is false.

VirginiA
Page 60
Williamsburg

WAshington
Page 62
Sonora Louise Smart Dodd started Father's Day.

West Virginia
Page 63
1. Weirton; 2. Ohio; 3. Weston; 4. Cheat; 5. Harper's Ferry;
6. Potomac; 7. Tug Fork; 8. Kentucky; 9. Charleston
Fact: The New River is America's oldest river.

WIsconsin
Page 64
1. B; 2. A; 3. R; 4. A; 5. B; 6. O; 7. O   (Baraboo)

WYoming

Canada
Page 67

Mexico
Page 68-69
1. Caribbean Sea; 2. Tijuana; 3. Tabasco; 4. Tortilla;
5. Rio Grande River; 6. Acapulco; 7. Mexicali; 8. Chihuahua;
9. Pacific Ocean; 10. Guatemala; 11. Ciudad Juárez; 12. El Paso
13. Belize; 14. Hermosillo
"Mexicans were once known as the men of corn."

T	G	R	P	P	H	B	L	S	T	I	Y	T
T	L	I	N	E	S	A	R	C	H	E	S	C
A	E	B	A	O	R	E	Z	Q	R	O	M	H
Z	N	N	T	P	D	I	N	O	S	A	U	R
R	C	O	U	L	E	N	N	B	K	I	R	I
O	A	O	R	E	F	G	S	G	N	T	A	S
L	N	T	A	O	E	X	D	O	Z	B	D	Q
N	Y	F	L	F	G	G	I	L	L	I	B	K
G	O	G	B	E	C	W	N	D	A	W	O	E
L	N	K	R	A	P	S	H	E	C	V	Y	N
A	S	T	I	R	D	O	U	N	H	R	R	D
D	D	A	D	T	E	N	D	S	B	O	C	R
E	T	E	G	H	V	P	L	P	A	I	H	A
N	X	R	E	O	Y	T	S	I	M	I	S	I
S	O	R	S	K	B	R	A	K	N	S	O	V
C	A	P	I	T	O	L	R	E	E	F	G	S
M	G	I	L	K	B	I	I	J	R	I	O	O
A	Q	R	L	E	B	S	H	O	A	O	N	O
O	J	C	R	A	Y	A	D	C	L	N	A	H
C	A	N	Y	O	N	L	A	N	D	S	P	C
T	A	H	H	R	N	I	M	L	A	W	M	I
R	C	A	L	E	X	S	Y	T	L	P	I	N
S	K	A	E	R	B	R	A	D	E	C	T	C

UTAH

labama
on page 8
ulation estimate: 4,447,100
: 50,750 sq. mi.
ertville B-4
xander City D-4
dalusia G-3
niston C-4
b B-3
ens A-3
hore G-2
ourn D-5
Minette G-2
semer C-3
rmingham C-3
az B-4
nt D-2
wton Bay G-2
nton D-3
lman B-3
eville G-4
atur A-3
nopolis E-1
chan G-5
erprise G-4
aula F-5
rence A-2
t Payne B-4
sden B-4
enville G-4
f Shores H-2
tersville B-4
milton B-1
over C-3
ntsville A-3
kson F-1
per D-5
ett D-5
ette G-2
bile H-1
nroeville F-2
ntgomery E-4
elika D-5
ark G-4
ark F-4
City C-4
nix City E-5
dmont B-4
hard G-1
anoke D-5
sellville A-4
ttsboro A-4
ma E-3
acauga D-4
adega C-4
assee E-4
omasville F-2
caloosa D-2
kegee E-4

laska
on page 9
ulation estimate: 626,932
570,374 sq. mi.
horage C-5
row A-5
hel C-4
banks C-5
mer D-5
eau D-5
kai D-5
chikan E-8
diak D-5
zebue B-4
me B-4
mer C-5

Petersburg D-7
Seward D-5
Sitka D-7
Soldotna D-5
Unalaska E-3
Valdez C-6

Arizona
Map on page 10
Population estimate: 5,130,632
Area: 113,642 sq. mi.
Ajo F-2
Apache Jct. E-3
Benson G-4
Bisbee G-5
Bullhead City D-1
Camp Verde D-3
Casa Grande F-3
Chandler E-3
Chinle C-5
Clifton F-5
Coolidge F-3
Cottonwood D-3
Douglas G-5
Eloy F-3
Flagstaff D-3
Florence F-3
Ganado C-5
Glendale E-3
Globe E-4
Grand Canyon C-3
Green Valley G-4
Holbrook D-4
Kayenta B-4
Kingman D-1
Lake Havasu City . . . D-1
Mesa E-3
Page B-3
Parker E-1
Payson E-3
Phoenix E-3
Prescott D-3
Prescott Val. D-3
Safford F-5
San Carlos E-4
Scottsdale E-3
Sedona D-3
Sells G-3
Show Low D-5
Sierra Vista G-4
Snowflake D-4
Somerton F-1
St. Johns D-5
Sun City E-3
Superior E-4
Tempe E-3
Tombstone G-5
Tuba City C-4
Tucson F-4
Wickenburg E-2
Willcox F-5
Williams D-3
Winslow D-4
Yuma F-1

Arkansas
Map on page 11
Population estimate: 2,673,400
Area: 52,075 sq. mi.
Arkadelphia F-3
Ashdown F-2
Batesville B-5
Bella Vista A-2
Benton C-4
Bentonville A-2
Blytheville A-7
Camden E-4

Clarksville B-3
Conway C-4
Crossett E-5
Dumas F-5
El Dorado E-4
Fayetteville A-2
Forrest City C-6
Fort Smith B-2
Harrison A-3
Heber Sprs. B-5
Helena C-6
Hope E-3
Hot Springs C-3
Jacksonville C-4
Jonesboro A-6
Little Rock C-4
Magnolia E-3
Malvern F-4
Marianna C-6
Mena C-2
Monticello E-5
Morrilton B-4
Mountain Home A-4
North Little Ro C-4
Osceola B-7
Paragould A-6
Pine Bluff F-5
Pocahontas A-6
Rogers A-2
Russellville B-3
Searcy B-5
Siloam Springs A-2
Springdale A-2
Stuttgart C-5
Texarkana E-2
Trumann B-6
Warren E-4
West Helena C-6
West Memphis B-7
Wynne B-6

California
Map on page 12
Population estimate: 33,871,648
Area: 155,973 sq. mi.
Anaheim I-6
Arcata B-1
Arroyo Grande H-3
Atascadero G-3
Auburn D-3
Bakersfield G-5
Barstow H-6
Berkeley E-2
Blythe I-8
Brawley I-7
Calexico J-7
Cambria G-3
Carlsbad I-6
Chico C-3
Chowchilla F-4
Chula Vista J-6
Clovis F-4
Coalinga G-4
Corning C-2
Delano G-5
El Centro J-7
Encinitas I-6
Escondido I-6
Eureka B-1
Fairfield E-2
Fort Bragg C-1
Fremont E-2
Fresno F-4
Gilroy F-3
Glendale H-5
Hanford F-4
Healdsburg D-2

Hollister F-3
Indio I-7
King City F-3
Lancaster H-5
Lemoore F-4
Lindsay G-5
Lodi E-3
Lompoc. H-4
Long Beach I-5
Los Angeles I-5
Los Banos F-3
Madera F-4
Manteca E-3
Marysville D-3
McFarland G-4
Merced E-4
Modesto E-3
Monterey F-3
Morro Bay G-3
Napa E-2
Needles H-8
Newport Beach I-6
Novato E-2
Oakland E-2
Oceanside I-6
Orland C-2
Oroville C-3
Oxnard H-5
Palm Springs I-7
Palmdale H-5
Palo Alto E-2
Paradise C-3
Pasadena H-5
Paso Robles G-3
Perris I-6
Placerville D-3
Pomona H-5
Porterville G-5
Red Bluff C-2
Redding B-2
Redlands H-6
Ridgecrest G-6
Riverside I-6
Roseville D-3
S. Lake Tahoe D-4
Sacramento D-3
Salinas. F-3
San Bernardino H-6
San Clemente I-6
San Diego J-6
San Francisco E-2
San Jose E-2
San Juan Capist I-6
San Luis Obispo G-3
Santa Ana I-6
Santa Barbara H-4
Santa Clarita H-5
Santa Cruz F-2
Santa Maria H-4
Santa Rosa D-2
Selma F-4
Soledad F-3
Stockton. E-3
Susanville C-3
Taft H-4
Tehachapi H-5
Thousand Oaks H-5
Tulare G-4
Turlock E-3
Twentynine Palms. . . H-7
Ukiah D-2
Vallejo. E-2
Ventura H-4
Victorville H-6
Visalia F-4
Vista I-6
Wasco G-4

Watsonville F-3
Willits C-1
Willows C-2
Woodland D-3
Yreka A-2
Yuba City D-3

Colorado
Map on page 14
Population estimate: 4,301,261
Area: 103,729 sq. mi.
Alamosa E-4
Arvada B-5
Aspen C-3
Aurora B-5
Boulder. B-5
Brighton B-5
Brush. B-6
Burlington C-7
Canon City D-5
Carbondale C-3
Castle Rock C-5
Colorado Springs . . C-5
Cortez E-2
Craig A-3
Delta C-2
Denver B-5
Durango. E-3
Englewood B-5
Estes Park. A-5
Fort Collins A-5
Fort Morgan B-6
Glenwood Sprs. B-3
Grand Junction C-2
Greeley A-5
Gunnison D-3
La Junta D-6
Lamar D-7
Leadville C-4
Littleton B-5
Longmont B-5
Loveland A-5
Manitou Sprs. C-5
Monte Vista E-4
Montrose D-2
Pueblo D-5
Rifle. B-3
Rocky Ford D-6
Salida D-4
Steamboat Sprin . . . A-3
Sterling A-7
Trinidad E-5
Vail B-4
Walsenburg E-5
Woodland Park C-5
Yuma B-7

Connecticut
Map on page 15
Population estimate: 3,405,565
Area: 4,845 sq. mi.
Bridgeport D-2
Bristol B-3
Danbury C-1
East Hartford. B-4
Fairfield D-2
Greenwich D-1
Groton C-5
Hamden C-3
Hartford B-3
Manchester B-4
Meriden C-3
Middletown C-4
Milford D-2
Mystic C-5
Naugatuck C-2
New Britain B-3

New Haven D-3
New London C-5
Norwalk D-2
Norwich. C-5
Putnam. A-5
Shelton D-2
Stamford D-1
Storrs B-5
Stratford. D-2
Torrington B-2
Trumbull D-2
Wallingford C-3
Waterbury C-2
West Hartford B-3
Willimantic. B-5

Delaware
Map on page 16
Population estimate: 783,600
Area: 1,955 sq. mi.
Bethany Beach F-3
Bridgeville E-1
Claymont A-2
Dover D-2
Georgetown E-2
Harrington. E-1
Laurel F-2
Lewes E-3
Middletown C-1
Milford E-2
Millsboro F-2
New Castle. B-1
Newark. B-1
Odessa C-1
Rehoboth Beach . . . E-3
Seaford F-1
Smyrna C-1
Wilmington A-2

District of Columbia
Map on page 7
Population estimate: 572,059
Area: 61 sq. mi.

Florida
Map on page 17
Population estimate: 15,982,378
Area: 53,937 sq. mi.
Apalachicola B-3
Arcadia E-6
Avon Park E-6
Bartow D-6
Belle Glade E-7
Blountstown B-3
Boca Raton F-8
Bradenton E-5
Brooksville C-5
Bunnell. C-6
Cape Canaveral. . . . D-7
Chipley A-3
Clearwater D-5
Clermont D-6
Clewiston E-7
Coral Gables G-7
Crestview A-2
Daytona Beach C-7
De Funiak Sprs. A-2
De Land C-6
Delray Beach F-8
Deltona C-6
Dunedin D-5
Fernandina Beach. . A-6
Fort Lauderdale . . . F-7
Fort Pierce E-7
Fort Walton Beach . B-2
Ft. Myers F-6

Index

Gainesville B-5
Hialeah F-7
Hollywood F-8
Homestead G-7
Immokalee F-6
Inverness C-5
Jacksonville B-6
Jacksonville Beach . B-6
Key Largo G-7
Key West H-6
Kissimmee C-6
Lake City B-5
Lake Wales D-6
Lake Worth F-8
Lakeland D-6
Leesburg C-6
Live Oak B-5
Marathon H-7
Marco F-6
Marianna A-3
Melbourne D-7
Miami F-7
Miami Beach F-8
Naples F-6
Ocala C-6
Orlando D-6
Ormond Beach C-7
Palatka B-6
Panama City B-2
Pensacola A-1
Perry B-4
Pompano Beach . . . F-8
Port Charlotte E-6
Port St. Joe B-3
Punta Gorda E-6
Quincy A-3
Sanford C-6
Sarasota E-5
Sebring D-5
Spring Hill D-5
St. Augustine B-6
St. Cloud D-6
St. Petersburg D-5
Starke B-6
Stuart E-7
Tallahassee A-3
Tampa D-5
Titusville C-7
Venice E-5
Vero Beach D-7
West Palm Beach . . E-8
Winter Garden D-6
Winter Haven D-6

Georgia
Map on page 18
Population estimate: 8,186,453
Area: 57,919 sq. mi.

Albany F-2
Americus E-2
Athens C-3
Atlanta C-2
Augusta D-4
Bainbridge G-2
Blakely F-1
Brunswick F-5
Cairo G-2
Calhoun B-1
Camilla F-2
Carrollton C-1
Cartersville C-1
Cedartown C-1
Columbus E-1
Cordele E-2
Dalton B-1
Dawson F-2
Douglas F-3

Dublin E-3
Eastman E-3
Elberton C-3
Fitzgerald F-3
Fort Valley E-2
Gainesville C-2
Griffin D-2
Hinesville F-5
Jesup F-4
La Grange D-1
Macon D-3
Marietta C-2
Martinez C-4
Milledgeville D-3
Monroe C-2
Moultrie F-2
Newnan D-1
Perry E-2
Plains E-2
Quitman G-3
Rome C-1
Roswell C-2
Sandersville D-3
Savannah E-5
St. Marys G-5
Statesboro E-5
Summerville B-1
Swainsboro E-4
Sylvester F-2
Thomaston D-2
Thomasville G-2
Thomson D-4
Tifton F-3
Toccoa B-3
Valdosta G-3
Vidalia E-4
Warm Springs D-1
Warner Robins E-3
Waycross F-4
Waynesboro D-4
Winder C-2

Hawaii
Map on page 19
Population estimate: 1,211,537
Area: 6,423 sq. mi.

'Aiea D-2
'Ewa D-2
'Ewa Beach D-2
Hau'ula B-3
Hilo D-6
Holualoa D-6
Honolulu D-3
Kahalu'u C-3
Kahului A-5
Kailua D-4
Kailua Kona D-5
Kamuela C-6
Kāne'ohe D-3
Kapaa A-2
Kekaha A-1
Kīhei A-5
Lahaina A-5
Lā'ie B-3
Lihue A-2
Mā'ili D-1
Mākaha C-1
Makawao A-6
Nānākuli D-1
Pearl City D-2
Pukalani A-6
Wahiawā C-2
Waialua C-2
Wai'anae C-1
Wailuku A-5
Waimānalo D-4
Waipahu D-2

Whitmore Village . . C-2

Idaho
Map on page 20
Population estimate: 1,293,953
Area: 82,751 sq. mi.

American Falls G-4
Arco F-4
Blackfoot G-4
Boise F-1
Bonners Ferry A-1
Buhl G-2
Burley G-3
Caldwell F-1
Challis E-3
Coeur d'Alene B-1
Emmett F-1
Gooding G-2
Grangeville D-1
Hailey F-3
Idaho Falls F-5
Jerome G-3
Kellogg B-2
Ketchum F-3
Lewiston C-1
McCall E-1
Montpelier H-5
Moscow C-1
Mountain Home . . . G-2
Nampa F-1
Orofino C-1
Payette F-1
Pocatello G-4
Preston H-5
Rexburg F-5
Rigby F-5
Rupert G-3
Salmon E-3
Sandpoint B-1
Soda Springs G-5
St. Anthony F-5
Sun Valley F-3
Twin Falls G-3
Weiser F-1

Illinois
Map on page 21
Population estimate: 12,419,293
Area: 55,593 sq. mi.

Alton F-2
Arlington Hts. A-5
Aurora B-4
Beardstown D-2
Belleville F-2
Benton G-4
Bloomington D-3
Canton C-2
Carbondale G-3
Carlinville E-3
Carmi G-4
Centralia F-3
Champaign D-4
Charleston E-4
Chester G-3
Chicago B-5
Chicago Hts. B-5
Cicero B-5
Clinton D-4
Collinsville F-2
Danville D-5
De Kalb A-4
Decatur D-3
Dixon B-3
Du Quoin G-3
E. St. Louis F-2
Effingham E-4
Elgin A-4

Evanston A-5
Fairfield F-4
Flora F-4
Freeport A-3
Galena A-2
Galesburg C-2
Geneseo B-2
Granite City F-2
Harrisburg G-4
Harvard A-4
Highland Park A-5
Hoopeston D-5
Jacksonville E-2
Jerseyville E-2
Joliet B-4
Kankakee C-5
Kewanee B-2
La Salle B-3
Lincoln D-3
Litchfield E-3
Macomb D-2
Marion G-4
Mattoon E-4
Mendota B-3
Metropolis H-4
Moline B-2
Monmouth C-2
Morris B-4
Mt. Carmel F-5
Mt. Vernon G-4
Naperville B-4
Nauvoo C-1
Normal C-3
Olney F-4
Ottawa B-4
Pana E-3
Paris E-5
Pekin C-3
Peoria C-3
Peru B-3
Pontiac C-4
Princeton B-3
Quincy D-1
Rantoul D-4
Rochelle A-3
Rock Falls B-3
Rock Island B-2
Rockford A-3
Salem F-4
Sandwich B-4
Springfield D-3
Sterling B-3
Streator C-4
Taylorville E-3
Urbana D-4
Vandalia F-3
W. Frankfort G-4
Waterloo F-2
Watseka C-5
Waukegan A-5
Wilmette A-5

Indiana
Map on page 22
Population estimate: 6,080,485
Area: 35,870 sq. mi.

Alexandria D-4
Anderson D-4
Angola A-6
Auburn B-5
Bedford F-3
Bloomington F-3
Bluffton C-5
Boonville H-2
Brazil E-2
Carmel D-3
Cedar Lake B-2

Charlestown G-4
Columbia City B-4
Columbus F-4
Connersville E-5
Crawfordsville D-2
Crown Point B-2
Decatur C-5
E. Chicago A-1
Elkhart A-4
Elwood D-4
Evansville H-1
Fort Wayne B-5
Frankfort D-3
Franklin E-4
French Lick G-3
Gary A-2
Goshen A-4
Greencastle E-2
Greenfield E-4
Greensburg E-4
Greenwood E-3
Hammond A-1
Hartford City C-5
Huntingburg G-2
Huntington C-5
Indianapolis E-3
Jasper G-2
Kendallville B-5
Kokomo C-3
La Porte A-3
Lafayette C-2
Lebanon D-3
Linton F-2
Logansport C-3
Madison G-5
Marion C-4
Martinsville E-3
Merrillville A-2
Michigan City A-2
Mishawaka A-3
Monticello C-3
Mount Vernon . . . H-1
Muncie D-5
Nappanee B-4
Nashville F-3
New Albany G-4
New Castle D-5
New Haven B-5
Noblesville D-4
North Vernon F-4
Peru C-4
Plymouth B-3
Portage A-2
Portland C-5
Princeton G-1
Rensselaer B-2
Richmond E-5
Rochester B-3
Rushville E-4
Salem G-3
Scottsburg G-4
Sellersburg G-4
Seymour F-4
Shelbyville E-4
South Bend A-3
Tell City H-2
Terre Haute E-2
Valparaiso A-2
Vincennes G-1
W. Lafayette C-2
W. Terre Haute E-1
Wabash C-4
Warsaw B-4
Washington G-2
Westville A-2
Winchester D-5

Iowa
Map on page 24
Population estimate: 2,926,3
Area: 55,875 sq. mi.

Algona . . . . B
Ames C
Anamosa C
Atlantic . . . . D
Bettendorf . . . . D
Burlington . . . . E
Carroll C
Cedar Falls C
Cedar Rapids C
Centerville . . . . E
Charles City . . . . . . B
Cherokee . . . . B
Clarinda . . . . E
Clear Lake . . . . B
Clinton C
Council Bluffs . . . . . D
Creston . . . . D
Davenport . . . . D
Decorah . . . . A
Denison C
Des Moines . . . . . . D
Dubuque . . . . B
Estherville . . . . A
Fairfield . . . . E
Fort Madison . . . . . E
Ft. Dodge . . . . B
Grinnell C
Harlan . . . . D
Independence . . . . B
Indianola . . . . D
Iowa City . . . . D
Iowa Falls . . . . B
Keokuk . . . . E
Knoxville . . . . D
Le Mars . . . . B
Manchester . . . . . . B
Maquoketa C
Marshalltown C
Mason City . . . . A
Mt. Pleasant . . . . . E
Muscatine . . . . D
Newton C
Oelwein . . . . B
Oskaloosa . . . . D
Ottumwa . . . . D
Pella . . . . D
Red Oak . . . . D
Shenandoah . . . . . E
Sioux City . . . . B
Spencer . . . . A
Storm Lake . . . . . . B
Vinton C
Washington . . . . . . D
Waterloo . . . . B
Waverly . . . . B
Webster City C
West Branch . . . . . D

Kansas
Map on page 25
Population estimate: 2,688,4
Area: 81,823 sq. mi.

Abilene C
Arkansas City . . . . . E
Atchison . . . . B
Beloit . . . . B
Chanute . . . . D
Colby . . . . B
Concordia . . . . B
Dodge City . . . . D
El Dorado . . . . D
Emporia . . . . D
Fort Scott . . . . D

Populations are 2000 census populations or latest available estima

den City D-2
rnett C-8
odland B-1
eat Bend C-4
ys C-4
tchinson D-5
lependence . . . E-7
a
action City B-6
nsas City B-8
ned C-4
wrence B-8
avenworth . . . B-8
eral E-2
nhattan
rysville A-6
Pherson C-5
wton D-5
rton A-3
athe B-8
tawa C-8
rsons D-8
sburg D-8
tt D-4
ssell C-4
ina C-5
ott City C-2
peka B-7
ysses D-1
ellington E-5
chita D-5
nfield E-6

entucky
p on page 26
ulation estimate: 4,041,769
a: 39,732 sq. mi.
hland B-8
rdstown C-5
rea D-6
wling Green . . . D-4
mpbellsville . . . D-5
rbin D-7
vington A-6
nthiana B-6
nville C-6
zabethtown . . . C-5
nkfort C-6
asgow D-4
rlan E-8
rrodsburg C-6
zard D-8
nderson C-3
pkinsville D-3
wrenceburg . . . C-6
banon D-5
xington C-6
ndon D-7
uisville C-5
disonville D-3
yfield E-2
ysville B-7
ddlesboro E-8
nticello E-6
rehead C-7
unt Sterling . . . C-7
rray E-2
vensboro C-3
ducah D-2
rtsville C-7
ris C-7
eville D-8
nceton D-2
hmond C-6
ssellville E-4
elbyville C-5
merset D-6

Williamsburg E-7
Winchester C-7

Louisiana
Map on page 27
Population estimate: 4,468,976
Area: 43,566 sq. mi.
Abbeville D-4
Alexandria C-4
Bastrop A-5
Baton Rouge D-5
Bogalusa C-7
Bossier City A-3
Bunkie C-4
Buras E-7
Chalmette D-7
Covington D-7
Crowley D-4
De Ridder C-3
Donaldsonville D-6
Eunice D-4
Franklin E-5
Grand Isle E-7
Hammond D-6
Houma E-6
Jeanerette D-5
Jennings D-4
La Place D-6
Lafayette D-5
Lake Charles D-3
Lake Providence A-5
Leesville C-3
Mansfield B-3
Marksville C-4
Metairie D-6
Minden A-3
Monroe A-4
Morgan City E-5
Natchitoches B-3
New Iberia D-5
New Orleans D-7
New Roads C-5
Oakdale C-4
Opelousas D-4
Plaquemine D-5
Ponchatoula D-6
Raceland E-6
Ruston A-4
Shreveport A-3
Tallulah A-5
Ville Platte C-4
Winnfield B-4
Winnsboro B-5

Maine
Map on page 28
Population estimate: 1,274,923
Area: 30,865 sq. mi.
Auburn F-1
Augusta F-2
Bangor E-3
Bar Harbor F-4
Bath F-2
Belfast F-3
Biddeford G-1
Brunswick G-2
Bucksport E-3
Calais D-5
Camden F-3
Caribou B-4
Dexter E-3
Dover-Foxcroft D-3
Eastport E-5
Ellsworth E-4
Fairfield E-2
Fort Kent A-4
Houlton C-4

Kennebunk G-1
Lewiston F-1
Lincoln D-4
Madawaska A-4
Madison E-2
Millinocket D-3
Norway F-1
Orono E-3
Pittsfield E-3
Portland G-1
Presque Isle B-4
Rockland F-3
Rumford E-1
Saco G-1
Sanford G-1
Skowhegan E-2
Van Buren A-4
Waterville E-2

Maryland
Map on page 29
Population estimate: 5,296,486
Area: 9,775 sq. mi.
Aberdeen A-5
Annapolis B-5
Baltimore B-5
Bowie B-5
Cambridge C-6
Columbia B-4
Crisfield D-6
Cumberland A-2
Easton C-6
Edgewood B-5
Frederick B-4
Hagerstown A-3
Laurel B-4
Lexington Park D-5
Ocean City D-7
Pocomoke City D-6
Reisterstown B-4
Rockville B-4
Salisbury D-6
Silver Spring B-4
St. Marys City D-5
Taneytown A-4
Waldorf C-4
Westminster A-4

Massachusetts
Map on page 30
Population estimate: 6,349,097
Area: 7,838 sq. mi.
Adams B-2
Amherst C-3
Athol B-4
Attleboro D-6
Boston C-6
Brockton D-6
Cambridge C-6
Chicopee C-3
Fall River E-6
Fitchburg B-5
Framingham C-6
Gardner B-4
Gloucester B-7
Great Barrington C-1
Greenfield B-3
Haverhill A-6
Holyoke C-3
Hyannis E-8
Lawrence B-6
Leominster B-5
Lexington B-6
Lowell B-6
Lynn B-7
Marlborough B-5
Medford B-6

Milford C-5
N. Adams B-2
New Bedford E-7
Newton C-6
Northampton C-3
Norwood C-6
Pittsfield B-1
Plymouth D-7
Provincetown D-8
Quincy C-6
Salem B-7
Southbridge D-4
Springfield D-3
Stoughton C-6
Taunton D-6
Ware C-4
West Springfield D-3
Westfield C-2
Weymouth C-7
Woburn B-6
Worcester C-5

Michigan
Map on page 32
Population estimate: 9,938,444
Area: 56,809 sq. mi.
Adrian H-7
Albion G-6
Alma F-6
Alpena D-7
Ann Arbor G-7
Battle Creek G-6
Bay City F-7
Benton Harbor H-4
Big Rapids F-6
Burton F-7
Cadillac E-5
Charlotte G-6
Cheboygan C-6
Coldwater H-6
Copper Harbor A-3
Detroit G-7
Escanaba C-4
Flint F-7
Frankfort D-5
Gaylord D-6
Grand Haven F-5
Grand Rapids F-5
Grayling D-6
Greenville F-6
Hastings G-6
Hillsdale H-6
Holland G-5
Houghton A-2
Ionia F-6
Iron Mtn. C-3
Ironwood B-1
Jackson G-6
Kalamazoo G-5
Lansing G-6
Lapeer F-7
Livonia G-7
Ludington E-4
Manistee E-4
Manistique C-5
Marquette B-3
Marshall G-6
Menominee D-3
Midland F-7
Monroe H-7
Mount Pleasant F-6
Muskegon F-5
Ontonagon A-2
Owosso F-7
Petoskey C-6
Pontiac G-8
Port Huron F-8

Portage G-5
Saginaw F-7
Sault Ste. Marie B-6
South Haven G-5
St. Johns F-6
St. Joseph H-4
Sturgis H-5
Tawas City E-7
Three Rivers H-5
Traverse City D-5
Warren G-8

Minnesota
Map on page 33
Population estimate: 4,919,479
Area: 79,617 sq. mi.
Albert Lea H-4
Alexandria F-2
Austin H-4
Bemidji D-2
Brainerd E-3
Cambridge F-3
Chisholm D-4
Crookston C-1
Detroit Lakes D-2
Duluth D-5
Ely B-5
Fairmont H-3
Faribault H-4
Fergus Falls E-1
Grand Marais C-6
Grand Rapids D-3
Hibbing D-4
Hutchinson G-3
International Falls B-4
Litchfield F-3
Little Falls E-3
Mankato H-3
Marshall G-2
Minneapolis G-4
Montevideo G-2
Moorhead D-1
Morris F-1
New Ulm G-3
Northfield G-4
Owatonna H-4
Park Rapids D-2
Pipestone H-1
Red Wing G-4
Rochester H-4
Silver Bay D-5
St. Cloud F-3
St. Paul G-4
St. Peter G-3
Thief River Falls C-1
Virginia C-5
Warroad B-2
Waseca H-3
Willmar F-2
Winona H-5
Worthington H-2

Mississippi
Map on page 34
Population estimate: 2,844,658
Area: 46,914 sq. mi.
Aberdeen C-5
Amory B-5
Batesville B-3
Biloxi H-4
Booneville B-5
Brookhaven F-2
Canton E-3
Clarksdale B-2
Cleveland C-2
Columbia G-3
Columbus C-5

Corinth A-5
Crystal Springs E-2
Forest E-4
Greenville C-2
Greenwood C-3
Grenada C-3
Gulfport H-4
Hattiesburg F-4
Holly Springs A-4
Indianola C-2
Jackson E-3
Kosciusko D-3
Laurel F-4
Leland C-2
Louisville D-4
McComb G-2
Meridian E-5
Natchez F-1
New Albany B-4
Oxford B-3
Pascagoula H-5
Philadelphia D-4
Picayune H-3
Richton F-4
Ripley A-4
Starkville C-4
Tunica A-2
Tupelo B-4
Vicksburg E-2
Waynesboro F-5
West Point C-5
Winona C-3
Yazoo City D-2

Missouri
Map on page 35
Population estimate: 5,595,211
Area: 68,898 sq. mi.
Aurora D-3
Bolivar D-3
Boonville B-4
Branson E-4
Cape Girardeau D-7
Carthage D-3
Caruthersville E-7
Charleston D-7
Chillicothe A-3
Clinton C-3
Columbia B-4
Dexter E-6
Farmington D-6
Fulton B-5
Hannibal B-5
Harrisonville C-3
Independence B-3
Jefferson City C-4
Joplin D-3
Kansas City B-3
Kennett E-6
Kirksville A-4
Lebanon D-4
Macon A-4
Malden E-6
Marshall B-4
Maryville A-2
Mexico B-5
Moberly B-4
Monett D-3
Neosho E-3
Nevada C-3
Osage Beach C-4
Park Hills C-6
Perryville D-6
Poplar Bluff E-6
Richmond B-3
Rolla C-5
Sedalia C-4

Index

Sikeston . . . . E - 7
Springfield . . . . D - 4
St. Charles . . . . B - 6
St. Joseph . . . . A - 2
St. Louis . . . . C - 6
Sullivan . . . . C - 5
Union . . . . C - 5
Van Buren . . . . D - 6
W. Plains. . . . . E - 5
Warrensburg . . . . . . C - 3

Montana
Map on page 36
Population estimate: 902,195
Area: 145,556 sq. mi.

Anaconda . . . . C - 3
Belgrade. . . . . D - 4
Billings . . . . D - 5
Bozeman . . . . D - 4
Butte. . . . . D - 3
Columbia Falls. . . . . A - 2
Conrad . . . . B - 3
Cut Bank . . . . A - 3
Deer Lodge . . . . C - 3
Dillon . . . . D - 3
Glasgow. . . . . A - 7
Glendive. . . . . B - 8
Great Falls . . . . B - 4
Hamilton . . . . C - 2
Hardin . . . . D - 6
Havre . . . . A - 5
Helena . . . . C - 3
Kalispell . . . . A - 2
Lewistown . . . . C - 5
Libby . . . . A - 2
Livingston. . . . . D - 4
Malta . . . . A - 6
Miles City . . . . C - 7
Missoula . . . . C - 2
Polson. . . . . B - 2
Roundup . . . . C - 5
Shelby . . . . A - 3
Sidney . . . . B - 8
Whitefish . . . . A - 2
Wolf Point . . . . B - 7

Nebraska
Map on page 37
Population estimate: 1,711,263
Area: 76,878 sq. mi.

Alliance . . . . B - 2
Auburn. . . . . D - 8
Aurora . . . . D - 6
Beatrice . . . . D - 7
Bellevue . . . . C - 8
Blair. . . . . C - 7
Broken Bow. . . . . . . C - 4
Chadron . . . . A - 2
Columbus. . . . . C - 6
Cozad . . . . D - 4
Crete . . . . D - 7
Fairbury . . . . D - 7
Falls City . . . . D - 8
Fremont . . . . C - 7
Gering . . . . B - 1
Gothenburg. . . . . . . C - 4
Grand Island . . . . . . C - 6
Hastings . . . . D - 6
Holdrege . . . . D - 5
Imperial . . . . D - 3
Kearney . . . . D - 5
Kimball. . . . . C - 1
Lexington . . . . D - 4
Lincoln . . . . D - 7
McCook . . . . D - 4
Minden. . . . . D - 5
Nebraska City . . . . . D - 8

Norfolk . . . . B - 6
North Platte . . . . C - 4
O'Neill. . . . . B - 5
Ogallala . . . . C - 3
Omaha . . . . C - 8
Plattsmouth . . . . C - 8
Schuyler . . . . C - 7
Scottsbluff . . . . B - 1
Seward . . . . C - 7
Sidney . . . . C - 2
Valentine . . . . A - 4
Wahoo . . . . C - 7
Wayne . . . . B - 7
West Point . . . . B - 7
York . . . . D - 6

Nevada
Map on page 38
Population estimate: 1,998,257
Area: 109,806 sq. mi.

Battle Mountain . . . B - 3
Beatty . . . . F - 3
Boulder City. . . . . . . G - 5
Caliente . . . . E - 5
Carson City. . . . . . . D - 1
Elko . . . . B - 4
Ely . . . . D - 5
Fallon . . . . C - 2
Hawthorne . . . . D - 2
Henderson . . . . G - 5
Las Vegas . . . . G - 5
Laughlin . . . . H - 5
N. Las Vegas. . . . . . G - 5
Reno . . . . C - 1
Sparks . . . . C - 1
Tonopah . . . . E - 3
Virginia City . . . . . . D - 1
Wells . . . . B - 5
Winnemucca . . . . . . B - 3
Yerington . . . . D - 2

New Hampshire
Map on page 39
Population estimate: 1,235,786
Area: 8,969 sq. mi.

Berlin . . . . C - 4
Claremont . . . . F - 2
Concord . . . . G - 3
Derry . . . . H - 4
Dixville Notch . . . . B - 4
Dover . . . . G - 5
Durham . . . . G - 5
Franklin . . . . F - 3
Hampton . . . . H - 5
Hanover . . . . E - 2
Jaffrey . . . . H - 2
Keene . . . . H - 2
Laconia . . . . F - 4
Lebanon . . . . F - 2
Littleton . . . . D - 3
Manchester . . . . G - 4
Milford . . . . H - 3
Nashua . . . . H - 4
Newport . . . . F - 2
North Conway. . . . . D - 4
Plymouth . . . . E - 3
Portsmouth . . . . G - 5
Rochester . . . . F - 5
Salem . . . . H - 4

New Jersey
Map on page 40
Population estimate: 8,414,350
Area: 7,419 sq. mi.

Asbury Park . . . . . . D - 5
Atlantic City. . . . . . . G - 4

Bayonne . . . . C - 4
Berlin . . . . F - 2
Bloomfield . . . . B - 4
Bridgeton . . . . G - 2
Browns Mills . . . . . . E - 3
Camden . . . . E - 2
Cape May . . . . H - 2
Cherry Hill . . . . E - 2
Clifton. . . . . B - 4
Edison . . . . C - 4
Elizabeth . . . . C - 4
Hackensack . . . . B - 5
Hammonton . . . . . . F - 3
Irvington . . . . C - 4
Jersey City . . . . C - 4
Lakewood . . . . E - 4
Linden . . . . C - 4
Long Branch . . . . . . D - 5
Margate City . . . . . . G - 3
Millville. . . . . G - 2
New Brunswick . . . . C - 4
Newark . . . . C - 4
Ocean City . . . . G - 3
Paramus . . . . B - 4
Passaic. . . . . B - 4
Paterson . . . . B - 4
Perth Amboy . . . . . . C - 4
Piscataway . . . . C - 3
Plainfield . . . . C - 4
Port Norris . . . . G - 2
Princeton . . . . D - 3
Ship Bottom. . . . . . . F - 4
Sussex . . . . A - 3
Toms River . . . . E - 4
Trenton. . . . . D - 3
Tuckerton. . . . . F - 4
Vineland. . . . . G - 2
Washington . . . . C - 2
Wayne . . . . B - 4
Wildwood . . . . H - 3
Williamstown . . . . . F - 2
Willingboro . . . . E - 2
Woodbury . . . . E - 2

New Mexico
Map on page 41
Population estimate: 1,819,046
Area: 121,364 sq. mi.

Alamogordo . . . . . . E - 3
Albuquerque . . . . . . C - 3
Artesia . . . . E - 4
Bloomfield . . . . B - 2
Carlsbad . . . . F - 5
Carrizozo . . . . D - 3
Clayton . . . . B - 5
Clovis . . . . D - 5
Deming . . . . F - 2
Espanola . . . . B - 3
Eunice . . . . F - 5
Farmington . . . . B - 1
Gallup. . . . . C - 1
Grants . . . . C - 2
Hobbs . . . . D - 5
Las Cruces . . . . F - 2
Las Vegas . . . . C - 4
Lordsburg. . . . . F - 1
Los Alamos. . . . . . . B - 3
Lovington . . . . E - 5
Portales . . . . C - 5
Raton . . . . A - 4
Roswell . . . . E - 4
Ruidoso . . . . E - 3
Santa Fe . . . . C - 3
Shiprock . . . . B - 1
Silver City . . . . E - 1
Socorro . . . . D - 2
Taos . . . . B - 3

Truth or Conseq . . . E - 2
Tucumcari. . . . . C - 5
Tularosa . . . . E - 3
Zuni . . . . C - 1

New York
Map on page 42
Population estimate: 18,976,457
Area: 47,224 sq. mi.

Albany . . . . E - 9
Albion. . . . . D - 4
Alexandria Bay . . . . B - 6
Amsterdam . . . . D - 9
Auburn . . . . D - 6
Batavia . . . . D - 4
Bath . . . . E - 5
Bay Shore . . . . H - 10
Binghamton. . . . . . . F - 5
Buffalo . . . . D - 3
Canandaigua . . . . . . D - 5
Canton . . . . A - 7
Cobleskill . . . . E - 8
Cooperstown . . . . . . E - 8
Cortland . . . . E - 6
Dansville . . . . E - 4
Dunkirk . . . . E - 2
East Hampton . . . . . G - 12
Elmira . . . . F - 5
Endicott . . . . F - 5
Fredonia . . . . E - 2
Freeport . . . . H - 9
Fulton . . . . D - 6
Geneseo . . . . E - 4
Geneva . . . . D - 5
Glens Falls . . . . D - 9
Gloversville . . . . D - 8
Hamburg . . . . E - 3
Herkimer . . . . D - 8
Hornell . . . . E - 4
Hudson . . . . E - 9
Ithaca . . . . E - 6
Jamestown. . . . . F - 2
Johnstown . . . . D - 8
Kingston . . . . F - 9
Lake George . . . . . . C - 9
Lake Placid . . . . B - 9
Lockport. . . . . D - 3
Malone . . . . A - 8
Massena . . . . A - 8
Merrick . . . . H - 9
Mexico . . . . C - 6
Middletown . . . . G - 8
Montauk . . . . G - 12
Monticello . . . . F - 8
New Rochelle . . . . . . H - 9
New York . . . . H - 9
Newark . . . . D - 5
Newburgh . . . . G - 9
Niagara Falls . . . . . . D - 3
Norwich . . . . E - 7
Ogdensburg. . . . . . . A - 7
Olean . . . . F - 3
Oneida . . . . D - 7
Oneonta . . . . E - 7
Oswego . . . . C - 6
Penn Yan . . . . E - 5
Plattsburgh . . . . A - 9
Potsdam . . . . A - 8
Poughkeepsie . . . . . F - 9
Riverhead. . . . . H - 11
Rochester . . . . D - 4
Rome . . . . D - 7
Salamanca . . . . F - 3
Saranac Lake . . . . . . B - 9
Saratoga Sprs. . . . . . D - 9
Schenectady. . . . . . . D - 9
Seneca Falls . . . . . . D - 5

Silver Creek . . . . E - 2
Syracuse . . . . D - 6
Ticonderoga. . . . . . . C - 9
Troy . . . . E - 9
Utica . . . . D - 7
Watertown . . . . B - 6
Watkins Glen. . . . . . E - 5
Wellsville . . . . F - 4
White Plains. . . . . . . G - 9
Yonkers . . . . H - 9

North Carolina
Map on page 44
Population estimate: 8,049,313
Area: 48,718 sq. mi.

Albemarle . . . . C - 5
Asheboro . . . . C - 5
Asheville. . . . . C - 2
Boone . . . . B - 3
Brevard . . . . C - 2
Burlington . . . . B - 5
Carolina Beach . . . . E - 7
Chapel Hill . . . . B - 6
Charlotte . . . . C - 4
Clinton . . . . C - 6
Concord . . . . C - 4
Dunn . . . . C - 6
Durham . . . . B - 6
Eden . . . . B - 5
Edenton . . . . B - 8
Elizabeth City . . . . . B - 8
Fayetteville . . . . C - 6
Forest City . . . . C - 3
Gastonia . . . . C - 4
Goldsboro . . . . C - 7
Greensboro . . . . B - 5
Greenville . . . . C - 7
Havelock . . . . D - 8
Henderson . . . . B - 6
Hendersonville . . . . C - 2
Hickory . . . . C - 4
High Pt. . . . . B - 5
Jacksonville . . . . . . D - 7
Kannapolis . . . . C - 4
Kinston . . . . C - 7
Kitty Hawk . . . . B - 9
Laurinburg . . . . D - 5
Lenoir . . . . B - 3
Lexington . . . . B - 5
Lincolnton . . . . C - 4
Lumberton . . . . D - 6
Monroe . . . . D - 4
Morehead City . . . . D - 8
Morganton . . . . C - 3
Mount Airy . . . . B - 4
New Bern . . . . C - 7
Newton . . . . C - 4
Oxford . . . . B - 6
Raleigh . . . . C - 6
Reidsville . . . . B - 5
Roanoke Rapids . . . B - 7
Rockingham. . . . . . . D - 5
Rocky Mount . . . . . . B - 7
Roxboro . . . . B - 6
Salisbury . . . . C - 4
Sanford . . . . C - 6
Shelby . . . . C - 3
Smithfield . . . . C - 6
Southern Pines . . . . C - 5
Statesville . . . . C - 4
Tarboro. . . . . B - 7
Washington . . . . C - 8
Waynesville . . . . C - 2
Whiteville . . . . D - 6
Williamston . . . . . . B - 8
Wilmington . . . . D - 7
Wilson . . . . C - 7

Winston-Salem . . . . B

North Dakota
Map on page 45
Population estimate: 642,20_
Area: 68,994 sq. mi.

Beulah C
Bismarck . . . . D-
Bottineau . . . . A
Bowman . . . . E
Carrington C
Crosby. . . . . A
Devils Lake . . . . B
Dickinson . . . . D
Ellendale . . . . E-
Fargo . . . . D
Grafton . . . . B
Grand Forks C
Harvey . . . . B
Hazen C
Hettinger . . . . E
Jamestown . . . . D
Langdon . . . . A
Linton . . . . E
Mandan . . . . D
Mayville C
Minot . . . . B
Rugby . . . . B
Valley City . . . . D
Wahpeton . . . . E
Watford City . . . . . . B
West Fargo. . . . . . . D
Williston . . . . B

Ohio
Map on page 46
Population estimate: 11,353_
Area: 40,953 sq. mi.

Ada . . . . D
Akron . . . . D
Alliance . . . . D
Ashland . . . . D
Ashtabula. . . . . B
Athens . . . . H
Barberton. . . . . D
Bellefontaine. . . . . . E
Bellevue C
Boardman . . . . D
Bowling Green C
Bryan . . . . B
Bucyrus. . . . . D
Cambridge. . . . . . . F
Canton . . . . D
Celina . . . . E
Chillicothe . . . . G
Cincinnati . . . . H
Circleville . . . . G
Cleveland C
Columbus . . . . F
Conneaut . . . . B
Coshocton . . . . F
Crestline . . . . D
Cuyahoga Falls . . . . G
Dayton . . . . G
Defiance C
Delaware . . . . F
Delphos . . . . D
Dover . . . . E
E. Liverpool . . . . . . E
Elyria C
Euclid . . . . B
Fairborn . . . . G
Fairport . . . . B
Findlay . . . . D
Fostoria . . . . D
Fremont C
Galion . . . . D
Gallipolis . . . . H

*Populations are 2000 census populations or latest available estima_*

neva . . . . B- 8
eenfield . . . . H- 3
eenville . . . . F- 1
milton . . . . H- 1
lsboro . . . . H- 3
nton . . . . J - 5
kson . . . . H- 5
nt . . . . D- 7
nton . . . . E- 3
ttering . . . . G- 2
ncaster . . . . G- 5
na . . . . D- 2
gan . . . . G- 5
ndon . . . . G- 3
rain . . . . C- 5
ansfield . . . . D- 5
arietta . . . . H- 7
arion . . . . E- 4
arysville . . . . F- 3
assillon . . . . D- 7
entor . . . . B- 7
ddletown . . . . . . G- 1
ount Gilead . . . . . E- 4
ount Vernon . . . . E- 5
poleon . . . . C- 2
w Lexington . . . . G- 5
w Philadelphia . . E- 7
wark . . . . F- 5
rwalk . . . . C- 5
rwood . . . . H- 1
ford . . . . G- 1
nesville . . . . B- 7
rma . . . . C- 6
qua . . . . F- 2
rt Clinton . . . . . . C- 4
rtsmouth . . . . . . I - 4
em . . . . E- 5
ndusky . . . . C- 4
aker Hts . . . . C- 6
elby . . . . D- 5
lney . . . . F- 2
ringfield . . . . . . F- 2
Marys . . . . E- 1
eubenville . . . . . E- 8
ongsville . . . . . . C- 6
nbury . . . . F- 4
fin . . . . D- 4
ledo . . . . B- 3
y . . . . F- 2
richsville . . . . . . E- 7
per Sandusky . . . F- 3
bana . . . . F- 3
n Wert . . . . D- 1
arren . . . . C- 8
ashington Cou . . . G- 3
auseon . . . . C- 2
ellston . . . . H- 5
esterville . . . . . . F- 4
nitehall . . . . F- 4
llard . . . . D- 4
lmington . . . . . . H- 2
ooster . . . . D- 6
nia . . . . G- 2
ungstown . . . . . . D- 8
nesville . . . . F- 6

klahoma
o on page 48
ulation estimate: 3,450,654
a: 68,679 sq. mi.
a . . . . C- 6
us . . . . C- 4
va . . . . A- 5
adarko . . . . C- 5
dmore . . . . D- 6
tlesville . . . . A- 7
ckwell . . . . A- 6

Boise City . . . . A- 1
Chickasha . . . . C- 5
Claremore . . . . B- 7
Clinton . . . . B- 4
Cushing . . . . B- 6
Duncan . . . . D- 5
Durant . . . . D- 7
El Reno . . . . B- 5
Elk City . . . . B- 5
Enid . . . . A- 5
Frederick . . . . D- 4
Guymon . . . . A- 2
Henryetta . . . . B- 7
Hugo . . . . D- 7
Idabel . . . . D- 8
Lawton . . . . C- 5
McAlester . . . . C- 7
Miami . . . . A- 8
Midwest City . . . . . B- 6
Muskogee . . . . B- 8
Norman . . . . C- 6
Oklahoma City . . . . B- 6
Okmulgee . . . . B- 7
Pauls Valley . . . . . . C- 6
Ponca City . . . . . . A- 6
Poteau . . . . C- 8
Pryor . . . . A- 8
Sallisaw . . . . B- 8
Seminole . . . . C- 6
Shawnee . . . . C- 6
Stillwater . . . . B- 6
Tahlequah . . . . B- 8
Tulsa . . . . B- 7
Vinita . . . . A- 8
Wagoner . . . . B- 8
Weatherford . . . . . . B- 4
Woodward . . . . A- 4

Oregon
Map on page 49
Population estimate: 3,421,399
Area: 96,002 sq. mi.
Albany . . . . B- 3
Ashland . . . . E- 3
Astoria . . . . A- 2
Baker City . . . . B- 7
Bend . . . . C- 4
Brookings . . . . E- 2
Burns . . . . D- 6
Coos Bay . . . . D- 2
Coquille . . . . D- 2
Corvallis . . . . B- 3
Cottage Grove . . . . C- 3
Dallas . . . . B- 3
Eugene . . . . C- 3
Florence . . . . C- 2
Grants Pass . . . . . . E- 3
Hermiston . . . . A- 6
Hillsboro . . . . B- 3
Hood River . . . . . . A- 4
John Day . . . . C- 6
Klamath Falls . . . . . E- 4
La Grande . . . . B- 7
Lakeview . . . . E- 5
Lebanon . . . . C- 3
Lincoln City . . . . . . B- 2
Madras . . . . B- 4
McMinnville . . . . . . B- 3
Medford . . . . E- 3
Milton-Freewater . . A- 6
Newberg . . . . B- 3
Newport . . . . B- 2
North Bend . . . . . . D- 2
Nyssa . . . . C- 7
Oakridge . . . . C- 3
Ontario . . . . C- 7
Oregon City . . . . . . B- 3

Pendleton . . . . A- 6
Portland . . . . B- 3
Prineville . . . . C- 5
Redmond . . . . C- 4
Reedsport . . . . C- 2
Roseburg . . . . D- 3
Salem . . . . B- 3
Seaside . . . . A- 2
Springfield . . . . . . C- 3
St. Helens . . . . A- 3
Stayton . . . . B- 3
Sutherlin . . . . D- 3
Sweet Home . . . . . C- 3
The Dalles . . . . . . A- 4
Tillamook . . . . B- 2
Warrenton . . . . A- 2
Winston . . . . D- 3

Pennsylvania
Map on page 50
Population estimate: 12,281,054
Area: 44,820 sq. mi.
Allentown . . . . D- 7
Altoona . . . . D- 4
Berwick . . . . C- 6
Bethlehem . . . . D- 7
Bloomsburg . . . . . . C- 6
Bradford . . . . A- 3
Butler . . . . C- 2
Carlisle . . . . D- 5
Chambersburg . . . . E- 4
Chester . . . . E- 8
Clarion . . . . C- 2
Clearfield . . . . C- 4
Coatesville . . . . . . E- 7
Connellsville . . . . . E- 2
Corry . . . . A- 2
Du Bois . . . . C- 3
E. Stroudsburg . . . . C- 8
Easton . . . . D- 8
Ephrata . . . . D- 6
Erie . . . . A- 1
Franklin . . . . B- 2
Gettysburg . . . . . . E- 5
Greenville . . . . B- 1
Grove City . . . . C- 1
Hanover . . . . E- 5
Harrisburg . . . . D- 6
Hazleton . . . . C- 7
Hollidaysburg . . . . D- 4
Huntingdon . . . . . . D- 4
Indiana . . . . D- 3
Johnstown . . . . D- 3
Kittanning . . . . C- 2
Lancaster . . . . E- 6
Latrobe . . . . D- 2
Lebanon . . . . D- 6
Lehighton . . . . C- 7
Lewisburg . . . . C- 5
Lewistown . . . . D- 5
Lock Haven . . . . . . C- 5
McKeesport . . . . . . D- 2
Meadville . . . . B- 1
Milford . . . . B- 8
Mt. Carmel . . . . . . C- 6
New Castle . . . . . . C- 1
Norristown . . . . . . E- 8
Oil City . . . . B- 2
Philadelphia . . . . . E- 8
Pittsburgh . . . . D- 1
Pottstown . . . . D- 7
Pottsville . . . . D- 6
Punxsutawney . . . . C- 3
Reading . . . . D- 7
Sayre . . . . A- 6
Scranton . . . . B- 7
Selinsgrove . . . . . . C- 6

Shamokin . . . . C- 6
Shippensburg . . . . . E- 5
Somerset . . . . E- 3
St. Marys . . . . B- 3
State College . . . . . C- 4
Stroudsburg . . . . . C- 8
Sunbury . . . . C- 6
Titusville . . . . B- 2
Tyrone . . . . D- 4
Uniontown . . . . . . E- 2
Upper Darby . . . . . E- 8
Warren . . . . B- 3
Washington . . . . . . D- 1
Waynesboro . . . . . E- 5
Wellsboro . . . . B- 5
Wilkes-Barre . . . . . C- 7
Williamsport . . . . . C- 5
York . . . . E- 6

Rhode Island
Map on page 51
Population estimate: 1,048,319
Area: 1,045 sq. mi.
Bristol . . . . C- 3
Cranston . . . . B- 2
E. Greenwich . . . . . C- 2
East Providence . . . B- 3
Greenville . . . . B- 2
Kingston . . . . D- 2
Newport . . . . D- 3
Pawtucket . . . . B- 3
Providence . . . . . . B- 3
Tiverton . . . . C- 3
W. Warwick . . . . . . C- 2
Warwick . . . . C- 3
Westerly . . . . D- 1
Woonsocket . . . . . A- 2

South Carolina
Map on page 52
Population estimate: 4,012,012
Area: 30,111 sq. mi.
Abbeville . . . . B- 2
Aiken . . . . C- 3
Anderson . . . . B- 2
Barnwell . . . . D- 3
Beaufort . . . . E- 4
Bennettsville . . . . . B- 5
Camden . . . . B- 4
Charleston . . . . . . E- 5
Cheraw . . . . B- 5
Chester . . . . B- 4
Clemson . . . . B- 2
Clinton . . . . B- 3
Columbia . . . . C- 4
Darlington . . . . C- 5
Dillon . . . . B- 6
Edisto Beach . . . . . E- 5
Florence . . . . C- 5
Folly Beach . . . . . . E- 5
Gaffney . . . . A- 3
Georgetown . . . . . D- 6
Greenville . . . . A- 2
Greenwood . . . . . . B- 2
Hartsville . . . . B- 5
Hilton Head Island . F- 4
Lake City . . . . C- 5
Lancaster . . . . B- 4
Laurens . . . . B- 3
Marion . . . . C- 6
Myrtle Beach . . . . . C- 6
N. Charleston . . . . . D- 5
Newberry . . . . B- 3
Orangeburg . . . . . . D- 4
Rock Hill . . . . A- 4
Seneca . . . . B- 1
Spartanburg . . . . . A- 3

Sumter . . . . C- 5
Union . . . . B- 3
Walterboro . . . . . . D- 4
York . . . . A- 4

South Dakota
Map on page 53
Population estimate: 754,844
Area: 75,896 sq. mi.
Aberdeen . . . . A- 6
Belle Fourche . . . . . B- 1
Brookings . . . . C- 8
Buffalo . . . . A- 1
Canton . . . . D- 8
Chamberlain . . . . . D- 5
Custer . . . . D- 1
Deadwood . . . . . . C- 1
Faith . . . . B- 3
Gettysburg . . . . . . B- 5
Hot Springs . . . . . . D- 1
Huron . . . . C- 6
Lead . . . . C- 1
Lemmon . . . . A- 3
Madison . . . . C- 8
Martin . . . . D- 3
Milbank . . . . B- 8
Mitchell . . . . D- 7
Mobridge . . . . A- 4
Pierre . . . . C- 5
Pine Ridge . . . . . . E- 2
Rapid City . . . . C- 2
Redfield . . . . B- 6
Sioux Falls . . . . . . D- 8
Spearfish . . . . C- 1
Sturgis . . . . C- 1
Vermillion . . . . E- 8
Wagner . . . . E- 6
Wall . . . . C- 3
Watertown . . . . . . B- 7
Webster . . . . A- 7
Winner . . . . D- 5
Yankton . . . . E- 7

Tennessee
Map on page 54
Population estimate: 5,689,283
Area: 41,219 sq. mi.
Athens . . . . B- 6
Bolivar . . . . B- 2
Brownsville . . . . . . B- 2
Chattanooga . . . . . C- 6
Clarksville . . . . A- 4
Cleveland . . . . C- 6
Columbia . . . . B- 4
Cookeville . . . . B- 5
Covington . . . . B- 1
Crossville . . . . B- 6
Dayton . . . . B- 6
Dickson . . . . B- 4
Dyersburg . . . . B- 2
Elizabethton . . . . . A- 8
Erwin . . . . A- 8
Fayetteville . . . . . . C- 4
Gallatin . . . . A- 5
Gatlinburg . . . . . . B- 7
Greeneville . . . . . . A- 8
Harriman . . . . B- 6
Humboldt . . . . B- 2
Jackson . . . . B- 2
Jefferson City . . . . . B- 7
Johnson City . . . . . A- 8
Kingsport . . . . A- 8
Knoxville . . . . B- 7
La Follette . . . . A- 7
Lawrenceburg . . . . C- 4
Lebanon . . . . A- 5
Lexington . . . . B- 3

Manchester . . . . . . B- 5
Martin . . . . A- 2
Maryville . . . . B- 7
McKenzie . . . . A- 2
McMinnville . . . . . . B- 5
Memphis . . . . C- 1
Milan . . . . B- 2
Morristown . . . . . . A- 7
Murfreesboro . . . . . B- 4
Nashville . . . . B- 4
Newport . . . . B- 7
Oak Ridge . . . . B- 6
Paris . . . . A- 3
Pulaski . . . . C- 4
Ripley . . . . B- 1
Rockwood . . . . B- 6
Savannah . . . . C- 3
Sevierville . . . . B- 7
Shelbyville . . . . . . B- 4
Springfield . . . . . . A- 4
Sweetwater . . . . . . B- 6
Tullahoma . . . . B- 5
Union City . . . . A- 2
Winchester . . . . . . C- 5

Texas
Map on page 56
Population estimate: 20,851,820
Area: 261,914 sq. mi.
Abilene . . . . D- 5
Alice . . . . G- 6
Alpine . . . . E- 3
Amarillo . . . . B- 4
Andrews . . . . D- 3
Aransas Pass . . . . . G- 7
Arlington . . . . C- 7
Athens . . . . D- 8
Atlanta . . . . C- 9
Austin . . . . E- 7
Bay City . . . . F- 8
Baytown . . . . E- 8
Beaumont . . . . E- 9
Beeville . . . . G- 6
Big Spring . . . . D- 4
Borger . . . . A- 4
Brady . . . . E- 5
Breckenridge . . . . . C- 6
Brenham . . . . E- 7
Brownfield . . . . C- 4
Brownsville . . . . . . H- 7
Brownwood . . . . . . D- 6
Bryan . . . . E- 7
Cameron . . . . E- 7
Canyon . . . . B- 4
Carthage . . . . D- 9
Childress . . . . B- 5
Coleman . . . . D- 5
Commerce . . . . C- 8
Conroe . . . . E- 8
Corpus Christi . . . . G- 7
Corsicana . . . . D- 7
Crockett . . . . D- 8
Crystal City . . . . . . F- 5
Cuero . . . . F- 7
Dalhart . . . . A- 3
Dallas . . . . C- 7
Del Rio . . . . F- 4
Denison . . . . C- 7
Denton . . . . C- 7
Dumas . . . . A- 4
Eagle Pass . . . . F- 5
Edinburg . . . . H- 6
El Campo . . . . F- 7
El Paso . . . . D- 1
Ennis . . . . D- 7
Fabens . . . . D- 1
Falfurrias . . . . G- 6

Index

Fort Stockton...... E-3
Fredericksburg..... E-6
Freeport.......... F-8
Ft. Worth........ C-6
Gainesville....... C-7
Galveston........ F-8
Gatesville........ D-6
Georgetown...... E-7
Gonzales........ F-7
Greenville........ D-8
Harlingen........ H-7
Henderson....... D-8
Hereford........ B-3
Hillsboro........ D-7
Hondo......... F-6
Houston........ F-8
Huntsville....... E-8
Jasper.......... E-9
Kermit......... D-3
Kerrville........ E-6
Kilgore......... D-8
Killeen......... E-6
Kingsville........ G-6
Lamesa........ C-4
Lampasas....... E-6
Laredo......... G-5
Levelland........ C-3
Littlefield........ B-4
Livingston....... E-8
Lockhart........ E-7
Longview........ C-8
Lubbock........ C-4
Lufkin......... D-8
Marshall........ C-9
Mathis G-6
McAllen........ H-6
Mexia D-7
Midland........ D-4
Mineral Wells C-6
Monahans....... D-3
Mt. Pleasant...... C-8
Nacogdoches...... D-8
Navasota E-8
New Braunfels..... F-6
Odessa......... D-3
Orange......... E-9
Palestine........ D-8
Pampa......... A-4
Paris C-8
Pearsall........ F-6
Pecos......... D-3
Perryton........ A-4
Plainview........ B-4
Pleasanton....... F-6
Port Arthur....... E-9
Port Lavaca...... F-7
Presidio......... F-2
Raymondville..... H-7
Rio Grande City.... H-6
San Angelo...... D-5
San Antonio...... F-6
San Marcos...... E-6
Seguin F-6
Seminole........ C-3
Sherman........ C-7
Sinton......... G-7
Snyder......... C-4
Stephenville....... D-6
Sulphur Springs.... C-8
Sweetwater D-5
Temple E-7
Terrell......... C-7
Texas City....... F-8
Tyler.......... D-8
Uvalde........ F-5
Vernon......... B-5
Victoria......... F-7

Waco........... D-7
Weatherford C-6
Wharton........ F-8
Wichita Falls C-6
Zapata......... H-5

Utah
Map on page 58
Population estimate: 2,233,169
Area: 82,168 sq. mi.
American Fork..... C-3
Blanding......... F-5
Bluff F-5
Bountiful B-3
Brigham City B-3
Cedar City F-2
Clearfield........ B-3
Ephraim D-3
Green River E-4
Heber City C-3
Helper......... D-4
Hurricane G-1
Kamas......... C-3
Layton......... B-3
Logan......... A-3
Manila......... B-5
Moab E-5
Murray......... C-3
Nephi D-3
Ogden......... B-3
Price.......... D-4
Provo......... C-3
Richfield E-3
Roosevelt C-4
Roy B-3
Salt Lake City..... C-3
Springville C-3
St. George G-1
Tooele......... C-2
Tremonton........ A-2
Vernal......... C-5
Wendover C-1

Vermont
Map on page 59
Population estimate: 608,827
Area: 9,249 sq. mi.
Barre.......... D-2
Bellows Falls F-2
Bennington G-1
Brattleboro G-2
Burlington C-1
Fair Haven E-1
Island Pond B-3
Manchester F-1
Middlebury D-1
Montpelier C-3
Newport........ B-3
Rutland......... E-1
South Burlington .. C-1
Springfield F-2
St. Albans B-1
St. Johnsbury C-3
Stowe C-3
Vergennes D-1
White River Jct..... E-3
Windsor E-3

Virginia
Map on page 60
Population estimate: 7,078,515
Area: 39,598 sq. mi.
Abingdon........ D-2
Alexandria A-7
Appomattox C-6
Arlington A-7
Bedford C-5
Blacksburg C-4

Bluefield........ C-3
Buena Vista C-5
Charlottesville B-6
Chesapeake D-8
Christiansburg C-4
Covington C-4
Culpeper B-6
Danville D-5
Emporia D-7
Farmville........ C-6
Franklin D-7
Fredericksburg..... B-7
Front Royal A-6
Galax.......... D-4
Hampton D-8
Harrisonburg B-5
Hopewell C-7
Lexington C-5
Lynchburg C-5
Manassas B-7
Marion D-3
Martinsville D-5
Newport News ... D-8
Norfolk........ D-8
Norton......... D-2
Petersburg C-7
Portsmouth D-8
Pulaski........ D-4
Radford C-4
Reedville........ C-7
Richmond....... C-7
Roanoke....... C-4
South Boston..... D-5
Staunton B-5
Stuarts Draft B-5
Suffolk........ D-8
Virginia Beach..... D-8
Waynesboro B-5
Williamsburg C-8
Winchester....... A-6
Woodbridge B-7
Wytheville D-3

Washington
Map on page 62
Population estimate: 5,894,121
Area: 66,581 sq. mi.
Aberdeen........ C-2
Anacortes........ A-3
Astoria E-2
Auburn......... C-3
Bellevue C-3
Bellingham A-3
Bremerton C-3
Camas......... E-3
Centralia........ D-3
Chehalis D-3
Chelan B-5
Clarkston D-8
Colville........ A-7
Ellensburg C-5
Ephrata........ C-6
Everett B-3
Goldendale D-5
Grandview D-5
Hoquiam C-2
Kennewick E-6
Longview........ E-2
Moses Lake C-6
Mt. Vernon B-3
Neah Bay B-1
Oak Harbor B-3
Olympia C-3
Omak B-6
Pasco......... D-6
Port Angeles B-2
Port Townsend ... B-3

Pullman D-8
Renton C-3
Richland D-6
Seattle C-3
Sedro Woolley.... A-3
Shelton C-2
Spokane......... B-7
Tacoma......... C-3
Toppenish D-5
Vancouver E-3
Walla Walla E-7
Wenatchee...... C-5
Yakima......... D-5

West Virginia
Map on page 63
Population estimate: 1,808,344
Area: 24,807 sq. mi.
Beckley......... F-3
Bluefield........ F-3
Buckhannon C-4
Charles Town..... C-7
Charleston E-2
Clarksburg C-4
Elkins D-5
Fairmont C-4
Grafton........ C-4
Harpers Ferry C-7
Huntington D-1
Keyser......... C-6
Lewisburg F-4
Madison E-2
Martinsburg..... C-7
Morgantown B-4
Moundsville..... B-3
New Martinsville.. B-3
Oak Hill E-3
Parkersburg C-2
Petersburg D-6
Princeton F-3
Pt. Pleasant D-1
Richwood...... E-4
Ripley........ D-2
Shinnston C-4
Summersville E-3
Weirton A-4
Welch F-2
Weston C-4
Wheeling B-3
White Sulphur Sprs. F-4
Williamson F-1

Wisconsin
Map on page 64
Population estimate: 5,363,675
Area: 54,314 sq. mi.
Antigo E-4
Appleton F-4
Ashland C-2
Baraboo F-3
Beloit G-4
Burlington G-4
Eau Claire E-2
Fond du Lac F-4
Green Bay E-5
Janesville G-4
Kenosha........ G-5
La Crosse F-2
Madison G-3
Manitowoc F-5
Marinette E-5
Marshfield E-3
Menomonie E-1
Merrill........ E-3
Milwaukee...... G-5
Monroe G-3
New London E-4
Oshkosh........ F-4

Platteville......... G-3
Portage.......... F-3
Prairie du Chien ... G-2
Racine.......... G-5
Rhinelander D-3
Rice Lake D-2
Richland Center... G-3
Shawano E-4
Sheboygan..... F-5
Sparta........ F-3
Stevens Point.... E-3
Sturgeon Bay.... E-5
Superior C-1
Tomah F-3
Two Rivers F-5
Waukesha G-4
Waupun G-4
Wausau E-3
West Bend F-4
Wisconsin Rapids .. E-3

Wyoming
Map on page 65
Population estimate: 493,782
Area: 97,105 sq. mi.
Buffalo A-5
Casper.......... C-6
Cheyenne....... E-7
Chugwater...... D-7
Cody A-3
Douglas C-6
Eden D-3
Edgerton B-6
Evanston E-2
Gillette A-6
Green River E-3
Jackson....... B-2
Kemmerer D-2
Lander C-4
Laramie E-6
Lyman E-2
Marbleton C-2
Moorcroft A-7
Newcastle B-7
Powell....... A-4
Rawlins D-5
Riverton C-4
Rock Springs .. E-3
Sheridan A-5
Thermopolis..... B-4
Torrington D-7
Wheatland D-7
Worland...... B-4

Canada
Map on page 66
Population estimate: 30,007,094
Area: 3,511,023 sq. mi.
Bella Coola....... E-1
Calgary F-2
Charlottetown..... F-8
Chibougamau F-7
Chicoutimi F-7
Dawson B-1
Edmonton E-2
Fort McMurray ... E-3
Fort Simpson ... C-2
Fredericton F-8
Grand Bank E-9
Halifax F-8
Hamilton G-6
Havre-St-Pierre .. E-8
Hay River D-3
Iqaluit........ C-6
La Loche E-3
London G-6
Lynn Lake E-4
Matagami F-6

Montréal .... G
Oshawa .... G
Ottawa .... F
Pickle Lake ...... F
Prince George ... E
Prince Rupert ... D
Québec......... F
Red Lake ...... F
Regina .... F
Rouyn-Noranda... F
Saint John ..... F
Saskatoon ..... F
Sherbrooke ..... G
St. Anthony ..... E
St. Johns ..... E
Sudbury ..... G
Thompson ..... E
Thunder Bay .... F
Toronto ..... G
Vancouver ..... E
Whitehorse C
Winnipeg ..... F
Yellowknife ..... D

Mexico
Map on page 68
Population estimate: 97,483
Area: 758,450 sq. mi.
Acapulco .... E
Aguascalientes ... D
Campeche ..... D
Cancún .... D
Chetumal ..... D
Chihuahua...... B
Ciudad Juárez ... A
Ciudad Obregón.. B
Ciudad Victoria ... C
Culiacán C
Durango...... C
Ensenada ..... A
Guadalajara..... D
Hermosillo .... B
La Paz C
León C
Los Mochis C
Matamoros C
Mazatlán C
Mèrida ...... D
Mexicali ..... A
Mexico City ... C
Monclova C
Monterrey C
Morelia...... C
Nuevo Laredo ... B
Oaxaca ...... E
Orizaba...... C
Pachuca C
Poza Rica .... D
Puebla .... D
Querètaro ..... D
Reynosa ..... B
Saltillo........ C
San Carlos C
San Felípe..... A
San Josè del Cabo. C
San Luis Potosì.. C
Tampico C
Tepic .... D
Tijuana ...... A
Torreón....... C
Tuxtla Gutièrrez .. D
Uruapan del Pro ... D
Veracruz...... D
Villahermosa ..... E
Xalapa .... D
Zacatecas C

Populations are 2000 census populations or latest available estimat